MINORITIES
AND
GIRLS
IN SCHOOL

LEADERS IN PSYCHOLOGY

———————•◆•———————

Series Editor
David Johnson

To make the research of the country's leading behavioral scientists accessible and to explain its meaning—those are the purposes of the **Leaders in Psychology** series. The chapters of the series began as seminars delivered on Capitol Hill in Washington, D.C. for members of Congress, their legislative staff members, and members of the Executive Branch of the Federal government. These people determine the science policies, not to mention much of the research funding, for the country. Yet almost none of them is a psychologist with a Ph.D. The challenge of the scientists who address them is to explain their research in terms that highly educated non-specialists will readily understand, and to go one step farther by considering the role of the research in addressing problems of national interest. In the **Leaders in Psychology** series, you have nothing less than the best psychological scientists telling you about their research and why it matters and doing so in words selected to illuminate.

Books in this series . . .

MINORITIES AND GIRLS IN SCHOOL

Effects on Achievement and Performance

DAVID JOHNSON
Editor

SAGE Publications
International Educational and Professional Publisher
Thousand Oaks   London   New Delhi

For information:

 SAGE Publications, Inc.
2455 Teller Road
Thousand Oaks, California 91320
E-mail: order@sagepub.com

SAGE Publications Ltd.
6 Bonhill Street
London EC2A 4PU
United Kingdom

SAGE Publications India Pvt. Ltd.
M-32 Market
Greater Kailash I
New Delhi 110 048 India

Printed in the United States of America

Library of Congress Cataloging-in-Publication Data

Main entry under title:

Minorities and girls in school: Effects on achievement & performance /
    edited by David Johnson.
      p. cm. — (Leaders in psychology; v. 1)
    Includes bibliographical references and index.
    ISBN 0-7619-0828-5 (cloth: acid-free paper). —
    ISBN 0-7619-0829-3 (pbk.: acid-free paper)
    1. Minorities—Education—United States. 2. Afro-Americans—
    Education. 3. School integration—United States. 4. Women—
    Education—United states. 5. Academic achievement—United States
    I. Johnson, David, 1949- . II. Series.
    LC3731.M5573 1997
    379.2'63—dc21   97-4857

97 98 99 00 01 02 03 10 9 8 7 6 5 4 3 2 1

Acquiring Editor:	C. Deborah Laughton
Editorial Assistant:	Eileen Carr
Production Editor:	Michèle Lingre
Production Assistant:	Denise Santoyo
Typesetter/Designer:	Janelle LeMaster
Cover Designer:	Candice Harman

Contents

Preface

———◆———

This country has a stake in educating its citizens well. Those it enables will produce for the country. Those it disables will find productivity difficult and may need to draw on national resources to survive. But the country has not been universally successful in enabling its citizens, though it is a national goal to do so. In particular, members of some ethnic and racial minority groups and girls have often found the social institutions in which they are educated to be obstacles, not aids, to enablement. Through much of our history, obstacles to enablement have been placed willfully before some citizens. It is also true that other obstacles have been inadvertent: For much of our history, we have not known in any scientific way what helps and what hinders the academic success of girls and minority group members. Taken together, those facts have made the relative lack of success of our schools in educating girls and minority students well both a scientific and a political issue.

This book gives voice to four of the psychologists who use scientific inquiry to understand what helps and what hinders the academic and life performance of minority students and girls. These are scientists who approach their subject matter with technical skill and personal passion. Theirs is not a dry, intellectual pursuit. It is a quest to build a reliable knowledge base about one of the most pressing social challenges of our time: to assure that an increasingly diverse citizenry will be ready to live and work successfully in the 21st century.

Rather than sequester their research from political scrutiny, Janet Schofield, Diana Slaughter-Defoe, Jacquelynne Eccles, and Nancy Betz have taken their findings to the heart of our political lives: Washington, D.C., and the U.S. Congress. Each of this book's four chapters began as a research briefing for members of Congress, their staff members, and other public officials in Washington. Each chapter represents an effort to communicate a vital area of scientific investigation to those in political life who could use that knowledge to formulate effective public policy. Near the end of each chapter are the questions that each of the authors was asked following the original briefing. These interchanges will give the reader a chance to see how policymakers begin to think about the use of scientific information in a political context. Perhaps their questions will stimulate your own desire to dig more deeply into the research. To aid your fulfillment of that desire, an excellent set of references is provided at the conclusion of each chapter.

Scientists talking to fellow scientists in their own subdiscipline share a language that is efficient but opaque to many who could profit from what they have to say. Schofield, Slaughter-Defoe, Eccles, and Betz here present their science in the words we all use. What they have to say will shock, edify, disappoint, and uplift you. It will leave you thinking about yourself, about your society, about human relations. It is living science.

· 1 ·

School Desegregation
40 Years After
Brown v. Board of Education

Looking Forward and Looking Backward

Janet Ward Schofield

ABOUT THIS CHAPTER

Desegregation. Few other social experiments of the past 40 years have so galvanized the nation. Idealists look to it as the tool to build a society free of racial prejudice, a society, in which opportunity is not restricted on the basis of one's race, ethnicity, or gender. Perhaps fearing just such an outcome, others have fiercely opposed it, and yet others have desired its intended outcome but have doubted that desegregation is truly the tool to bring about equality of opportunity and a racially harmonious society.

1

Janet Schofield is one of a handful of scientists who have asked where the truth lies. What has desegregation accomplished? She and her colleagues have looked with an unblinking scientific eye at this phenomenon, and they have found that desegregation's effects have been many because in practice, desegregation is itself many things. In some instances, its effects have been magnificent, creating both opportunity and solid working relationships among members of different races. In other instances, desegregation has been no more than segregation in a smaller space. What science has to offer to the understanding of complex social experiments is the ability to tease the pieces apart and make sense of what seem to be inconsistent outcomes. Science, as Janet Schofield will show you, has the power to explain how public policies can achieve their purposes. Sadly, she will also make clear that the study of effects of desegregation is largely a thing of the past. Our country's policies have turned away from concerted efforts to achieve gender and racial equity, even though the job is far from finished.

———————— •◆• ————————

I want to tell you about three interrelated issues. First, I will provide a brief historical overview of the policy of school desegregation to set the context for thinking about it as a current social issue. Second, I will discuss some bottom-line conclusions that can be drawn from the hundreds of studies on how school desegregation, as it has been implemented in this country, has influenced students' academic and social outcomes. And third, I'd like to make some observations about what we have learned about the process of interracial schooling from recent research. This latter discussion is very important for us today because, whether or not specific desegregation plans are upheld by the courts, increasing diversity in our society means that a larger and larger number of schools are going to have very heterogeneous student bodies. So finding workable answers to questions about how to make such schools really constructive environments for all the students involved should be a very urgent issue on our national agenda.

A Brief History of Desegregation

Let me turn to the first issue, the history of desegregation. For our purposes, school desegregation began in 1954 with the now famous Supreme Court decision, *Brown v. the Board of Education* (1954). That decision overturned the earlier doctrine that was propounded in the *Plessy v. Ferguson* case, that separate but equal public facilities for Blacks and Whites could be mandated by state law. The Brown decision argued instead that segregation in the schools, and I quote here, "generates a feeling of inferiority [in Black children] that may affect their hearts and minds in ways unlikely ever to be undone" (p. 2).

Thus, enforced segregation of the schools by race was seen to violate the equal-protection clause of the Constitution (Read, 1975; Wisdom, 1975) and to provide inherently unequal educational opportunities. The *Brown* decision, and later attempts to implement it, raised a storm of controversy that is easily forgotten or overlooked by people who were not immediately involved with it. (Edelman, 1973; Hochschild, 1984; Kluger, 1976) White resistance to the policy was expressed in an extraordinary number of ways ranging from physical attacks on Black students to the opening of separate so-called segregation academies to the occasional shutting down of entire public school districts to avoid desegregating them (Bell, 1980; Kluger, 1976; Smith, 1965).

This resistance stymied efforts to achieve desegregation for a full 10 years after the 1954 decision. Thus, in 1964, about 98% of Black children in the South were still going to all-Black schools (Holsendolph, 1976; Jaynes & Williams, 1989). Things changed in the mid-1960s, however, with passage of the Civil Rights Act in 1964 and the Elementary and Secondary Education Act in 1965. These two laws gave some teeth to the Court's decision. Substantial desegregation occurred between 1965 and 1973, most especially in the South. The majority of schools in the South were characterized by what was called *de jure segregation*, that is, state-mandated dual school systems of the kind specifically dealt with by the *Brown* decision.

In sharp contrast, very little change occurred during that time in the North. For example, the proportion of Black students in predominantly White schools in the North shifted almost imperceptibly in those 8 years, from 28% to 29% (Feagin, 1980). National statistics today show that the current amount of desegregation is remarkably, and discouragingly from some points of view, similar to that achieved back in 1973. This isn't to say there haven't been changes in specific cities and specific regions, but it is to say that increases in desegregation of certain areas have been balanced by decreases in other regions (Orfield, 1983; Orfield, Monfort, & Aaron, 1989).

The stability of national statistics notwithstanding, there are three very, very important changes since 1973 that must be mentioned.

First, when desegregation was initially conceived and implemented, the students involved were, for the most part, White or African American. This is not the case today. In this era, an increasing number of school districts are struggling to serve very diverse student bodies.

Second, and to some extent as a consequence of the first development, numerous large urban school districts are experiencing increasing difficulty creating and maintaining desegregated schools in the original sense of that word, that is, schools in which there are substantial numbers of Whites and substantial numbers of Black students. Differential minority and majority immigration and birthrates, differential uses of private schools, and a differential flow of White and minority families to the suburbs, have led to increasing racial and ethnic isolation in many cities. Although "White flight" from desegregated schools appears to account for a little bit of this change, the increasing concentration and isolation of minority groups in large urban centers is also a very pronounced and a very common pattern in cities such as New York and Chicago where there are no mandatory desegregation plans (Armor, 1988; Rossell, 1990).

The third major change that has occurred since 1973, a change not reflected in desegregation statistics, is a fairly major, although perhaps superficial, shift in public attitudes toward desegregation. The shift among Whites has been dramatic (Taylor, Sheatsley, & Greeley, 1978). Between 1942 and 1982, the percentage of Whites giving to survey researchers a response supportive of the principle of school desegregation, that is, the principle that Blacks and Whites should go to school together, rose 58 percentage points. What this indicates is a strong shift toward favorable attitudes about the principle of desegregation at a general, ideological level. The shift when it comes to nitty-gritty implementation plans has been much less dramatic. So for example, although there has been some increase in acceptance of cross-district busing to achieve desegregation, that increase in acceptance is minuscule compared to the increase in acceptance of the general principle of desegregation.

Unlike Whites, African Americans as a group initially showed strong support for the principal of desegregation and have done so consistently. Beginning in the early 1970s, however, a substantial number of African Americans began to express negative attitudes about implementation issues. More recently, a number of eminent African Americans have begun to question whether school desegregation as a strategy is the most effective way for African Americans to achieve effective education for their children (Bell, 1980; Blakey, 1989; Edmonds, 1980; Hamilton, 1968; Sampson & Williams, 1978; Sizemore, 1977).

I think this shift in emphasis is partly related to the demographic shifts that I mentioned earlier. It has become increasingly apparent that large numbers of African American children are likely to remain in racially isolated schools. Another important contributing factor is an awareness that African Americans have disproportionately borne the burdens of desegregation (Arnez, 1978; Sizemore, 1978). That is, studies show that African Americans have disproportionately been fired when staffs were merged, that Black children were more likely to be bused than White children, and that Black schools were more likely to be closed than predominately historically White schools (Butler, 1974; Hamilton, 1968; Haney, 1978; Orfield, 1975; Spruill, 1966).

It takes no special insight for me to tell you there is little reason to expect widespread political support for new mandatory desegregation. Recent Supreme Court decisions about affirmative action and existing desegregation plans alone make that very clear. However, the fact remains that very large numbers of children from minority and majority groups alike are now in racially and ethnically heterogeneous schools, and they are likely to remain there. The challenge to make schools with diverse student bodies work as effectively as possible for all those children is one that it is in our best interest to face.

As I mentioned earlier, the *Brown* decision laid the legal foundation for school desegregation based on the constitutional principle of equal protection. But for most people, majority and minority alike, the

5

immediate and pressing issue was precisely how desegregation was likely to affect children and especially their own children. It was this widespread concern that led to a very substantial amount of research on the effects of desegregation.

That brings us to the heart of our discussion: an examination of what we know from 40 years of research about the impact of school desegregation on academic and social outcomes for students.

What We Know From 40 Years of Research on Desegregation

Near-Term Outcomes for African Americans

The outcome that has received the most research attention is the academic achievement of minority students, specifically the academic achievement of African American students. You will notice from the first that I will rarely make reference to studies that deal with students from other minority backgrounds. The reason is that little research has been done on the impact of desegregation on minority groups other than African Americans. I can't tell you about something that doesn't exist.

I am aided in my discussion by the fact that since 1975, there have been 12 separate reviews of the literature on the effects of school desegregation on academic achievement. There is great variation in scope among these reviews. Some of them include hundreds of studies; some include only small numbers of methodologically strong studies. Several of these reviews were done as a group around 1984 (Cook et al., 1984). In that year, officials at the National Institute of Education (NIE)—which has now become of the Office of Educational Research and Improvement—at the Department of Education decided they wanted to see if a consensus could be built about what the impact of desegregation was on the academic achievement of minority students. So they pulled together a panel of scholars of very different backgrounds and outlooks and got them to agree to work together. They were to come up with some agreed-on methodological criteria and, using those criteria, to pick a group of studies that would be subjected to a statistical technique called *meta-analysis*. I won't go into the technical detail of how this is done. Suffice it to say that meta-analysis is a procedure that permits one to accumulate the results of disparate studies. So rather than looking one by one at a set of studies and trying to figure out without the help of statistics what they are all saying, meta-analysis allows one to combine the studies mathematically and extract from them some overall conclusions.

I think the analysis of the 1984 NIE group is useful and well done. So, for what follows, I will rely heavily on their analysis. 1984 may sound a little old to you. But the fact is that there hasn't been a significant amount of research done on our topic since that time. Moreover, the results have stood up well over time.

The first conclusion from the analysis is that desegregation has a positive impact on the reading ability of African American students. The estimate of how big this impact is varies from one study to another. It is fair to say, however, that the studies, which were mostly 1 year in length, suggest a gain equivalent to about 2 to 6 weeks of progress in reading achievement. That is, students in desegregated schools come out at the end of the year 2 to 6 weeks ahead of where it was anticipated they would be had they been in a nondesegregated environment.

In contrast, there seems to be little evidence of gains in mathematics. That is, the performance of African American children in desegregated schools is not different from the performance of African American children in nondesegregated schools. Reading and math are the two areas that were most frequently examined in the research probably because they are the two areas that have been of most concern to the public. Before leaving the topic of academic performance, I should mention that a number of the reviews suggest the impact of desegregation on achievement is greatest in the earliest grades. That is, the impact may well be greater in kindergarten through third grade than it is in succeeding years.

Near-Term Outcomes for Whites

What of the impact of desegregation on the performance of White children? What emerges from the research is that desegregation does not appear to harm the academic achievement of White students—as opponents of the process often fear and claim it might. This finding seems solid. There aren't as many studies of this issue as there are of the impact of desegregation on African American achievement, but there are many of them, and the overwhelming majority show no impact in either direction for White students. That is, there is no academic benefit as measured by tests of reading and mathematics ability, but there is also no academic loss. When statistically significant results do occur, they tend to be more positive than negative. The typical result, however, is no impact at all.

Medium-Term and Long-Term Impacts of Desegregation

Although changes in standardized test scores are one very common way to judge the impact of desegregation on academic performance, there are other equally important outcomes that deserve our attention. I will look at two of them: student drop-out rate and college enrollment. There is much less information on these topics than on reading and math performance, but I will summarize what we do know. With regard to student drop-out rate, the research suggests that African American students in desegregated schools are less likely to drop out of high school than are those who are not in desegregated schools. In fact, the researchers on one of these studies, Crain and Weisman (1972), make the flat statement that, and I'm quoting here, "integration seems to reduce the drop-out rate by about one fourth" (p. 156). A few studies suggest that Hispanic drop-out rates are lowered by attendance at desegregated schools, especially when those schools offer a major bilingual program. So there is at least some evidence that the drop-out rate is positively affected by desegregated schooling.

There is also some reason to think that desegregation encourages minority students to achieve more positive outcomes in their later lives than they might have otherwise. By positive outcomes later in life, I am talking about things such as occupational attainment. I should add that researchers have just begun to study outcomes of this kind.

Two researchers who have done a lot of work in this area, Braddock and Dawkins (1984), argue that desegregation may have long-term social and economic consequences for minorities through a number of mechanisms. I am going to mention just a few of them.

They argue that desegregated schooling can lead to access. It aids the building of social networks that, in turn, can provide useful job information, contacts, and sponsorship. Second, they point out that the desegregated environment can foster development of interpersonal skills on the part of both minority and majority group individuals. Those skills may make people more willing to seek employment in mixed contexts. These researchers note that survey research shows that employers sometimes hold a negative attitude toward graduates of predominantly Black institutions. That attitude places students coming out of African American institutions at a disadvantage. Attendance at desegregated schools helps African American students avoid those negative attributions and increases the number of job possibilities open to them (Braddock, 1980; Braddock & McPartland, 1982; Crain, 1970; Crain & Weisman, 1972; McPartland & Crain, 1980).

As I said, this area of investigation is relatively new and the body of research is not yet large, but there is reason to think from the research that is available that there are some positive impacts later in life of having been educated in a desegregated environment. There is some research, for example, that suggests graduates of integrated high schools are more likely to move into careers that have been traditionally closed to African Americans. Many of these careers are somewhat higher paying than those that have been open for, and popular among, African Americans. The research also shows that Black graduates of integrated institutions who have gone into the labor market tend to have an advantage over their peers who have gone to predominantly Black institutions. That advantage may derive in part from their being somewhat protected from the negative employer attitudes toward graduates of Black institutions that has been revealed by surveys (Braddock, Crain, McPartland, & Dawkins, 1986). There is also evidence to indicate that education in a desegregated setting has a positive impact on the types of college education and the number of years of college education that African Americans undertake (Braddock, 1985). To summarize, it appears that desegregation has a positive, although modest, effect on postsecondary education choices, on the variety of jobs for which African Americans are able to compete successfully, and on earnings.

The Impact of Desegregation on Intergroup Relations

Although most research on desegregation has focused on its effects on academic achievement, there is a fairly large body of work on the impact of desegregation on intergroup relations, specifically on inter-racial attitudes. Although many of those concerned with desegregated schools tend to be relatively uninterested in how integrated schooling affects intergroup relations, I think there are compelling reasons to give very serious thought to this issue.

I would just observe to begin with that social learning occurs in schools whether or not it's planned. Thus, an interracial school can-not but have an effect on intergroup relations. The choice, rather, is whether it will have a planned or an unplanned effect. Even a laissez faire policy concerning intergroup relations sends a message, either that school authorities are satisfied with the current state of those relations or that they don't feel the nature of intergroup relations is a legitimate concern for educational institutions. I believe authorities who argue that schools shouldn't attempt to influence intergroup relations miss the really fundamental fact that they are having an effect on intergroup relations whether or not they set out to do so (Schofield, 1982). Because of the pervasive residential segregation in our society, students frequently have their first extended contact with those from different racial or ethnic groups in the schools. Hence, whether stereo-typing and hostility grow or diminish is likely to be critically influ-enced by the particular experiences that children have in those schools.

I acknowledge that there is still a major difference of opinion about whether the development of close interracial ties should be a high priority in this country. Even so, there is at least a growing awareness of the very real costs of intergroup hostility and stereotyping. For example, a commission set up during the Bush administration sub-mitted a major report to the Secretary of the Department of Labor in 1991. It stated that working with people of culturally diverse back-grounds is now one of the five basic competencies required of Ameri-can workers. The report actually urged schools to try to teach this competency (Secretary's Commission, 1992).

The impact of intergroup relations is far-reaching. Not only do such relations affect possibilities in the work place, they can also affect academic achievement (Braddock & McPartland, 1987; Crain, 1970; Katz, 1964; McPartland & Crain, 1980; Pettigrew, 1967; Rosenberg & Simmons, 1971; U.S. Commission on Civil Rights, 1967). Katz's (1964) work, for example, suggests that the academic performance of African

American children can be markedly impaired in biracial situations where there is a major social threat to those children. And the potential constructive effect of positive intergroup relations on minority group outcomes is highlighted by some work of Braddock and McPartland (1987). They found that Black high school graduates who used desegregated social networks in their job searches were likely to obtain positions with higher salaries than those who used segregated social networks. Perhaps it is no surprise that these students were also more likely to end up working in environments that have, on average, a larger proportion of White workers.

Having argued that intergroup relations have a significant impact and that desegregation can influence the quality of such relations, let us turn to the research evidence for my claim. There is less work in this area than in the area of academic achievement, but the research that does exist suggests that, in the long run, desegregation helps in a small but important way to break the cycle of racial isolation. In this cycle, both minority and majority group members, unused to contact with each other, avoid each other despite the fact that this may limit their social, occupational, or residential choices. Two studies, for example, suggest that increasing levels of school desegregation are related to decreasing amounts of residential segregation (Pearce, 1980; Pearce, Crain, & Farley, 1984). At the individual rather than the community level, there are findings that support the idea that individuals who have attended desegregated schools are more likely to report living in integrated neighborhoods when they are adults (Crain, 1984; Crain & Weisman, 1972). They also report having social contacts with people from other racial and ethnic backgrounds, again, when they are adults. It is also true that individuals who attend desegregated high schools are more likely to have work associates from the other groups than those who haven't gone to these kinds of high schools (Green, 1981, 1982). Braddock, Crain, and McPartland (1984) have summarized the results of several national surveys, and they conclude that Black graduates of desegregated schools are more likely to end up working in desegregated environments than their peers who attended segregated schools.

There is little comparable research on the impact of desegregation on Whites, but what there is suggests a parallel kind of finding. Moreover, there is some evidence that, in the long run, desegregation in schools decreases overall segregation in the society and helps to break down some of the social and attitudinal barriers that keep minority group members from participating fully in the social and economic life of the broader community.

The research on the long-term impact of school desegregation is small compared to the volume of work on the impact of school desegregation on short-term racial attitudes. There are dozens of studies on this short-term impact. I won't tell you about each of them. Rather, I will give you the bottom-line result from this research. The bottom line is that the studies leave the question of the impact of desegregation on racial attitudes without a clear answer. A large group of studies shows an improvement; a substantial number of studies show no change; and there are studies that show increasingly negative attitudes accompanying desegregation.

What Is to Be Learned From Inconsistent Results Regarding Racial Attitudes?

You could find these results very discouraging. You could throw up your hands and say, "We haven't learned anything." I don't see it that way. I think these studies tell us a lot. The wide variation in those results highlights the point that social psychologists interested in desegregation have made again and again during the more than 40 years since Gordon Allport (1954) published a book called *The Nature of Prejudice*. In that book, published the same year as the *Brown* decision, Allport argued that contact between majority and minority group members can result in either an improvement in intergroup relations or a deterioration in such relations. What makes the critical difference is the nature of the contact situation, the way in which the contact is structured.

Desegregation Is Not Just an Event; It Is a Process

Let me lay out the essence of Allport's argument and draw out some of its implications for racially mixed schools. Before I do that, I want to make a point that is consistent with Allport's argument. My point is that desegregation is a process more than an event. It is true that desegregation is an event—an often controversial one that causes substantial organizational change—in the sense that there is a point in time where desegregation begins. Achieving that beginning often requires a tremendous marshaling and coordinating of resources. Both achieving the court order or other political or legal support required to bring about school desegregation and getting to the day desegregation actually begins in a school district have been so complicated and so demanding of time and effort and resources that many have been happy to regard desegregation as an event. School district officials have often acted as if once the student body was racially mixed, then school desegregation had, in fact, been accomplished. The event was over, and now they could just go ahead and carry on with business as usual. The fact is, however, that for the teachers, the students, the parents, and the school administrators, the act of mixing students racially in a school has been just the first step in a long-term process. And what is achieved ultimately in desegregating each school is heavily dependent on what happens during that long-term process.

School desegregation is, in many ways, like finding a job. Both involve a protracted period of preparation. Both may involve extensive negotiation between parties whose interests are partially, although not completely, compatible. Both often involve significant life changes. Yet with all of this, you aren't likely to have a successful career or contribute much to your employer's goals if, after signing the contract that gives you the job, you say, "Well, that's done," and settle back and do nothing more. The signing of the contract is, in fact, the beginning of the job. It is what happens after that that will determine whether the job accomplishes the purposes of the employer and the employee.

So, one of today's take-home messages is that it is crucial to pay attention to the process of desegregation and to the structuring of that process if desegregation is to accomplish its purposes.

To Desegregate, You Have to Desegregate

Let me, therefore, say something about aspects of the process that are very important. In taking up this topic, I will be circling back to Allport shortly. The first question to ask of a desegregated school is, has the desegregation actually created a racially mixed environment? That may sound like an odd question. But the fact is that a desegregated school can easily replicate racial isolation and stratification within its supposedly mixed student body. How can you have a desegregated school that isn't desegregated? Well, it is perfectly possible for a school that has a very diverse ethnic and racial makeup to simultaneously be an institution in which individuals of various groups have no contact with each other, or next to none. I'm sure many of you know this from your own experience. The segregation that occurs in desegregated schools can be extreme. In one school that I know of, researchers wanted to talk with Black and White students. The White students would talk with the researchers at lunch, and the Black students would talk with them at lunch. But the researchers couldn't talk with both groups of students at lunch simultaneously because the students wouldn't sit at the same table.

So here you have a desegregated school that, in fact, has two separate racial streams. One student summed up this kind of situation wonderfully, I thought, when he said, "All the segregation in the city is now in this one school." So the first point on process is that, to have a chance of being effective, a desegregated institution really needs to be desegregated. It can't be two segregated institutions operating inside the walls of one.

How does this resegregation occur? There are a number of common educational practices that lead, often inadvertently, to partial, or even substantial, resegregation. The most obvious of these are the very widespread practices that are designed to reduce academic heterogeneity within classes. These practices are generally labelled as *ability grouping* or *tracking*.

Let me hasten to add, however, that school policies are far from the only source of resegregation. It is undeniable that students voluntarily resegregate themselves to an extraordinary degree. My story about the researchers who couldn't talk simultaneously to Black and White students illustrates this phenomenon. The extent of such voluntary resegregation can be remarkable. I recognize that there is nothing inherently wrong with students who share a particular interest or value or background associating with each other to achieve valued ends. To the extent, however, that the grouping by race within a desegregated school reflects hostility, or anxiety, or discomfort, it is incumbent on those responsible for the school to act decisively. This is not a grouping around a shared interest. It is a grouping that threatens the success of the desegregation effort. The importance of avoiding a pattern of resegregation within schools is made clear by the work of many social psychologists, but I will mention only the work of Tajfel (1970). His research shows that when individuals are divided into groups, they tend to favor the in-group and discriminate against the out-group even though these groups have no history of antipathy or isolation or even prior relationships.

Thus, if you create or encourage racially and ethnically homogeneous groups, your social policy will resegregate students. The consequence is that already existing tendencies toward discrimination and stereotyping are likely to be magnified by these groupings, even when there had been no preexisting history of conflict that could have led to the discrimination and stereotyping. The tendency itself is common. Grouping helps the tendency to become active.

So great care needs to be taken to avoid school policies that lead to resegregation. Just as important, schools need to adopt policies that undercut student tendencies to cluster in racially homogeneous groups because of fear or uncertainty.

The Quality of Relations in Desegregated Schools Also Counts

Now, the mere absence of resegregation within a desegregated school is not enough to create an atmosphere or a set of circumstances that fosters constructive rather than destructive relationships between students from different backgrounds. The quality of the relationship is the crucial factor, not just the fact that there is some contact or there is some relationship. And if there is one thing that both social psychological theory and everyday experience have taught us in the last 30 or 40 years it is that simply putting people from different backgrounds together is not enough to ensure positive social outcomes.

So what should the schools do to try to create an environment that is conducive to positive social outcomes? Well, there are a great many specific actions that can help accomplish this objective. But rather than presenting you with a laundry list of 52 surefire strategies, many of which might not suit situations of interest to you, it is more valuable for me to tell you about the principles that underlie effective strategies. And to do that, I will rely on the thinking of Gordon Allport regarding the means to improve intergroup relations.

Some Guidance on Positive Intergroup Relations From Gordon Allport

Allport (1954) argued in *The Nature of Prejudice* that there are three aspects of contact situations that are particularly important in determining whether positive intergroup relations are likely to develop. These aspects are (a) equal status within the context of the situation, (b) an emphasis on cooperative activities within that situation, and last, (c) the very clear support of authorities in the situation for positive, equal-status relationships.

Equal-Status Relationships

I will talk about each of these aspects in turn. First, Allport argued that the contact situation should be structured in a way that gives equal status to all groups. There are a variety of mechanisms for doing this. I will mention just a few. In a school, as in just about every organization, the various positions people fill are ordered in what a sociologist might call a *status hierarchy*. That is, the people at the top have authority over the people at the middle level, and the people at the middle level have authority over people at the lower level. The challenge in a desegregated school is to see that members of all groups are distributed throughout the status hierarchy rather than being concentrated at a particular level.

Among the students, one phenomenon that occurs regularly makes achieving this distribution difficult. It is that one often finds in desegregated schools that the White students come from more educated and affluent backgrounds than do the minority students. There is, in effect, a preexisting status hierarchy from richer to poorer and from having many educational opportunities to having fewer such opportunities. And the hierarchy is stratified along racial and ethnic lines. This reality poses a serious challenge for schools that are trying to achieve equal status. And the school can exacerbate the situation. If, for example, the school tracks students on the basis of test scores, it may well end up with heavily White, high-status, accelerated groups and heavily minority, low-status, regular groups. When this happens, students are not only resegregated, but they are resegregated in a way that reinforces traditional stereotypes.

16

The problem is not necessarily solved by choosing not to track. If the school decides not to track at all, then it may end up with minority children who have formal equal status in the sense that they share the same classrooms with White students. But those same minority children may have an informal low status because they themselves recognize, and their White classmates may recognize as well, that their academic work may be weaker than that of their White peers (Orfield, 1975).

Hence, schools concerned about creating an equal-status environment that find themselves dealing with a student body in which the students as groups enter with different levels of performance have a very, very difficult problem with which to deal. I don't think that anyone has come up with a wholly satisfactory resolution to the problem, but there are some creative partial solutions available now, and a number of psychologists and sociologists have been working to find additional ways to deal with this issue. I will address some of them in the upcoming discussion on creating cooperative environments. Although it may not be possible initially to achieve informal equal status among the students, the image of status that is presented to them is important to consider. If the principal, the assistant principal, and the master teachers are all White and the teacher aides are all Black, that sends a message about status. At the very least, a school needs to strive to place people of the backgrounds represented in the student body at the various status levels in the school hierarchy. At some point, students should be taught by teachers who are of their background.

Cooperative Relationships

To foster positive intergroup relations, Allport (1954) argued that in addition to creating a situation that gives different groups equal status, it is also extremely important that the activities in which the individuals engage have a strong cooperative rather than competitive element to them. There are at least two reasons for this. First, given that discrimination is both historical fact and a present reality in many spheres of life, it is probable that placing students in competitive activities will support preexisting unconstructive stereotypes. There is a second reason for supporting cooperative over competitive activities. It is at least as compelling as the first reason. It is this: There is considerable research showing that competition between groups can lead to stereotyping, and I'm not talking majority and minority groups here but rather people who come from identical social backgrounds! This stereotyping can lead to unwarranted devaluation of the other group's accomplishments and to marked hostility, even when the groups involved have no initial history that might predispose them to have negative reactions to each other. The research shows that there is just something about the competitive process that sets these negative stereotypes, devaluations, and hostilities in motion (Sherif, Harvey, White, Hood, & Sherif, 1961). If even people from the same background begin to devalue each other when they are in competition, it is reasonable to expect that the effect will be magnified when people from very different backgrounds are placed in competition.

Both theory and research suggest that the kind of cooperation most likely to lead to the reduction of intergroup tensions or hostility is cooperation toward achieving a shared goal that cannot be achieved through the efforts of one group alone (Sherif et al., 1961). Researchers have developed and carefully field-tested several approaches to academic work that meet this criterion. These approaches have been demonstrated time and time again to improve achievement of lower-achieving students without slowing the progress of more advanced students. They also quite clearly foster positive attitudes toward out-group members. In the structuring of cocurricular or extracurricular activities, such as the production of school plays, the composition of sports teams, or the membership of clubs, schools have another excellent opportunity to create a cooperative environment. Thus, we do have some tools to help schools that wish to do so foster the kind of cooperation that Allport's (1954) initial theorizing, and 40 years of subsequent research, suggest are very useful in improving intergroup relations. I would add that by fostering positive regard for out-group members and by raising the achievement levels of lower-achieving students, good cooperative programs can go some of the way toward fulfilling Allport's first principle, that of creating an equal-status atmosphere for positive intergroup relations.

Support of Authority for Positive Relationships

Allport's third principle is that the support of authority, law, and custom for equal-status, positive relationships among members of all groups is very important if positive changes in intergroup attitudes and behavior are to be produced as a result of contact between those groups.

Now, certainly, a court ruling that requires desegregation is an important sign of support of government for desegregation. In and of itself, however, it isn't nearly enough. For the school child, the most relevant authorities are the school principal, the teachers, and, of course, the parents. And for some children, religious leaders can also be important authorities. The importance of a principal in a desegregated school can hardly be overemphasized. The principal plays at least four important roles in supporting the outcome of intergroup relations.

First, principals play an enabling function. That is, they make choices that facilitate or impede efforts to improve intergroup relations: How will scarce time and money be used? Will teachers be encouraged to try cooperative strategies?

Second, they serve a modeling function. It is clear that many people, not everybody but many people, tend to emulate authority. And the principal can set a model of behavior for teachers and students. Of course, there is no guarantee that everyone is going to follow the principal's example, but certainly, it is helpful if the principal's behavior exemplifies the behavior that is expected in the school.

Third, the principal can play a sensitizing function. The principal is in a good position to argue for the importance of paying attention to the quality of intergroup relations and to put this issue in an important place on the schools' agenda.

Last, principals can serve a sanctioning function. That is, they can actively reward positive practices and behaviors and discourage negative ones. As I indicated earlier, principals aren't the only relevant authorities in the school. Teachers are vital authority figures as well, and just as the principal can influence outcomes through enabling, modeling, sensitizing, and sanctioning, so too can the teachers.

The "Color-Blind" Approach to Support by Authorities

To finish my discussion of Allport's third principle, I want to consider a controversial issue. It is common for authorities in a desegregated school—principals, teachers, and parents—to feel the best and fairest thing they can do is to adopt the point of view that is sometimes called *the color-blind perspective.* This perspective sees racial and ethnic group membership as irrelevant to the ways individuals are treated. Taking cognizance of group membership in decision making is perceived as illegitimate and likely to lead to either discrimination against minority group members or reverse discrimination against majority group members. Two considerations make serious thought about the operation of the color-blind perspective in desegregated schools very worthwhile. The first consideration is that the color-blind perspective is widely held. It is to be found not only in desegregated schools but in other areas of our economic and social life as well. It is a frequently espoused goal in employment, judicial decisions, and the like. The second consideration is that even though the color-blind perspective is very appealing, and it is consistent with the long-standing American emphasis on the importance of the individual, it also leads very easily to misrepresentation of reality in ways that are likely to encourage discrimination against minority group members.

Before discussing further these negative aspects of the color-blind perspective, I want to acknowledge that in the desegregated schools I have seen, the color-blind perspective does have some positive consequences. In the short term, it seems to tamp down the potential for overt racial or ethnic conflict by generally de-emphasizing the salience of race and encouraging evenhanded application of the rules. It also sometimes seems to mitigate the discomfort or anxiety people feel in a new situation by saying to them that they don't have to deal with the race issue.

Despite these positive qualities, the color-blind perspective has some negative consequences that require serious examination. The most important of these, as I've mentioned, is that the perspective can make it easy to adopt without much examination or thought policies that are disadvantageous to minority groups. Let me give you a couple of examples. In a school that I studied, the suspension rate for Black students was roughly four times that for White students. Because this was a color-blind school, any question of why this was the case and whether the suspension policy was fair were not seen as legitimate questions. The administrators and faculty insisted they dealt with students as individuals and could do nothing about the disproportionate number of Black students who happened to be suspended.

From my point of view, it was important for that school to consider what was causing that disproportionate suspension rate and to examine whether the school's legitimate need for discipline could be met without creating a situation where the suspension rate for different groups was so disproportionate. In this case, school policies were underscoring inequalities between groups. The school's perspective prevented a cooperative effort to achieve a more balanced policy, and school authorities were not supportive of efforts to acknowledge, let alone to address, the problem.

Another simple incident will further illustrate some of the dangers inherent in a color-blind perspective as it operates in a school. This is a case where a White teacher in a school that adhered very strongly to the color-blind perspective deliberately miscounted votes in a student council election. The result was that a child the teacher characterized as "responsible," a White male, was declared the winner over a Black girl who was characterized as "unstable" by the teacher. The Black girl actually had a few more votes. The teacher seemed very uncomfortable with her action when I talked with her about it. But the focus of the concern was her subversion of the democratic process. As far as I could tell from a very extended conversation with her, she didn't consciously consider the races of the individuals involved. She also didn't consider the fact that her actions had changed the racial composition of the student council. The proportion of Black students on the student council was already low compared with their proportion in the school, and the teacher's action made that situation worse. In fact, 3 months later, the issue of Black underrepresentation on the student council became a bone of contention in the school.

So, in this case, the school's color-blind policy made it easy for the teacher to avoid recognizing the full implications of her behavior. She thought only about whether she had treated individuals fairly. Although she knew she hadn't, she decided that her rationale for taking this action justified it. She didn't think about group outcomes or group consequences of her behavior. She didn't recognize that her actions contributed to setting up the circumstances for the later contention over Black underrepresentation on the student council.

Let me be clear about what I am saying about the color-blind perspective. I am not suggesting that principals and teachers should constantly remind students of their group membership and make it salient minute by minute, day by day. There is strong evidence that constantly making group membership salient reinforces out-group hostility and discrimination. What I am suggesting is that it is important for school system administrators, principals, and teachers to recognize that, in racially or ethnically mixed schools, students understand their environments not just as interpersonal environments, not just as environments in which there are mixtures of individuals, but also as intergroup environments in which individuals are also members of groups. That being the case, those involved with the education of students need to be sensitive not just to individual outcomes but also to group outcomes.

So, What Have We Learned?

I will close by reminding you of some of the more important points of this discussion. First, it is fair to say on the basis of more than 40 years of research that desegregation has numerous positive outcomes. It improves the academic achievement of African Americans in the area of reading, an area that is fundamental to most other academic areas. It appears to have positive, long-term educational and occupational consequences for minority students. It does not appear to pose a threat to the academic achievement of White students, as many individuals fear. Moreover, it can provide majority and minority students with interpersonal skills and attitudes that will be of value to them as participants in the social and economic life of our increasingly pluralistic society.

Achieving these outcomes, however, is not easy. The challenge for those involved in desegregated schools is to take very seriously the proposition that desegregation is not just an event. It is an ongoing process that requires careful thought and planning to assure that all students are well served. The schools will best be able to serve all their students if they take account of the knowledge that has been generated by years of research. Among the messages that research has generated are these: Avoid resegregation; foster equal status and cooperation between students from different racial and ethnic backgrounds; and make it very clear that those in authority fully support policies that stimulate positive intergroup relations. Achieving the positive effects of desegregation may not be easy, but it is possible—if careful attention is paid to process.

———•◆•———•◆•———•◆•———

Q: *You mentioned that the bulk of research had been done on African Americans and Whites. I am curious about what research you think is needed with respect to groups other than African Americans? Where are the gaps in knowledge?*

A: I think what we need now is more work that helps us understand some of the process issues that I was talking about. The political and legal environments are such now that I don't think it is either feasible or fruitful to turn research toward comparing court-ordered plan A to court-ordered plan B. Instead, it would be better to go to the school level, that is, go into the classrooms and get to know the issues that arise at racially and ethnically heterogeneous schools. If the issues are identified, then we can ask process questions about the handling of those issues. How are decisions about those issues made? Who are the decision makers? How can the issues best be handled?
Understanding the processes in multiethnic and multiracial schools would be valuable not only for informing social policy but also for helping us understand the nature of relationships in such settings and the means to assure that the relationships will be positive.

Consider how concerned the country is with violence in the schools and how little we know about the contribution of relationships among heterogeneous groups to that violence. I think there may be a difference between the nature of violence in a heterogeneous versus a homogeneous setting. In a homogeneous setting, the causes and the consequences of violence are likely to be interpersonal. In the heterogeneous setting, disputes or animosities that might begin as conflicts between one person and another can spiral into conflicts between the groups from which the original disputants sprang. Understanding the nature of these processes and how they differ between homogeneous and heterogeneous environments could be very helpful. We really don't know enough about those dynamics in complex multiracial and multiethnic student bodies.

Let me just say that one reason we know so little about these environments is that the bulk of the research was done before 1975. It was the heyday of desegregation. Most of the schools that had major desegregation plans built those plans around Whites and African Americans, not all the different racial and ethnic groups that populate schools today. Since that time, there has been neither major research funding support nor a social atmosphere supportive of such research. The result is that our cities and our schools have changed dramatically in the past 20 years, but researchers have not been able to follow those changes closely nor to isolate the issues that arise as a particular consequence of heterogeneity. You asked where the gaps in knowledge are. They are everywhere.

Q: *I enjoyed your presentation and the structure of your presentation very much. One of the disadvantages of speaking on Capitol Hill, of course, is that you may be subject to questions that are on people's minds that particular week. I work for Congressman John Conyers, and one thing that is on his mind, and I think is also on the minds of a lot of the other members of the Black Caucus, is the threat to historically Black colleges and universities (HBCUs) right now, both locally and federally. I just wanted to hear your view about higher education and how some of your findings on desegregation in primary and secondary schools correlate to the data on higher education, because as it is right now, most of the bachelor's degrees that are being conferred on African Americans are coming from the HBCUs. At the same time, some research says that students at these institutions tend to believe they are performing better academically than they actually are. But then, you can look at the White institutions and you see that many of them provide a counterproductive learning environment for Black students. I was hoping that you could address that mixed picture if not with data, then maybe with theory.*

A: The impacts of different higher education settings is not the area of my research expertise. So rather than speaking from research or theory, I will speak from experience. I used to teach at Spellman College, which, as many of you know, is a very fine Black women's college. Having taught there, and also having at least passing familiarity with the issues you have raised, I see HBCUs as serving a very important function. Moreover, I don't think that view is contradictory to the arguments I have been making.

One important thing that differs between segregated primary and secondary schools and HBCUs is choice. That is, if you are an African American and you choose to go to a certain kind of institution when you could have chosen some other option, that is a very different thing from being forced to attend a particular school simply because of the color of your skin. The ability to choose an educational institution that meets your needs is fundamentally different from being coerced to attend a school that does not meet your needs. The old-fashioned dual school systems were symbolic of a certain power relationship. Such systems sent a message to African Americans that White people had the power and they could use that power to maintain separation between the races. That isn't what HBCUs are about, and it isn't what a choice to attend an HBCU is about.

I want to return to my time as a teacher in an HBCU. I got to know a lot of the students during that time. That experience has led me to form two opinions. On the one hand, I think those institutions are useful and valuable. But I also think that it is very important for individuals at some point in their formative years, whether they are White or African American or Hispanic or whatever, to be in situations where they do have substantial exposure to people from groups other than their own. Here is the experience that led me to form that view. I can remember specific individuals whom I knew at Spellman who were offered what they considered—not just what I considered, what they considered—very good jobs in "White" banks or other similar business institutions. And they chose not to take them. Why? Because they had completely segregated experiences up through college and including college. It was just too much of a change in their social environment to move in their first job into an environment that was almost exclusively White. These young people gave up many thousands of dollars in potential additional earnings, and I often think they gave up an

equivalent amount in terms of long-term social mobility and in terms of future job prospects because they were afraid of moving into a largely non-Black environment. I understand the reason for their reticence. The fact that they had lived exclusively in one kind of environment contributed strongly to it. This makes me think people need to spend time in environments that help them learn how to deal effectively with people who are not of their own race or ethnicity. That is not the same as saying that Black institutions should not exist. I am just saying that along with a choice to attend a Black college, a student should also make a choice to take advantage of opportunities to interact with non-Black people. I also have reservations about Whites going to entirely White institutions for their full education. Such single-race environments provide a less rich and varied
social experience than is required to produce socially well-rounded individuals who are ready to live and function productively in a multiracial, multiethnic country and world. One really needs to take full advantage of the opportunities that are available. So that is my opinion. It is not research based. It did, however, arise from substantial reflection on my experiences.

Q: *The large urban school districts of today face problems that, it seems to me, are unlike those faced in the 1970s when major desegregation was taking place. Students in these schools are from many racial and ethnic backgrounds; indeed, many are recently arrived from other countries. I suppose there aren't many Whites in these schools. The urban schools also tend to have a lot of low-income students, and the school districts themselves are strapped for cash so that they can't afford to do lots of creative things. How does the notion of desegregation fit into the situation of these poor, multiethnic, multiracial, inner-city schools?*

A: My research in the last few years has not been on the plight of those in these schools. So let me say that there are others who could answer this question better than I can. That said, I agree with the concern that is behind your question. Given the situation in many urban districts, such as Chicago, it becomes unrealistic to say, "Let's put all our eggs in the desegregation bas-

ket." You are not often going to see the case where an urban
district is going to go out to the suburbs to find White kids to
bring into the inner city to achieve racial balance. By the same
token, it may not be feasible to send really large numbers of the
minority-group kids in such cities out to heavily White suburban schools. However, if it is not possible to desegregate, it is
also not enough to say simply, "Well, so be it." You have many
thousands of kids in urban schools that are not going to be desegregated in any meaningful way. You can't just throw up your
hands in exasperation and walk away from the challenge. You
have to ask, "How do we address the needs of these kids productively in their current educational setting?"

I have no illusion about how difficult it is to answer that
question well because I have playing in the back of my head the
findings of the old U.S. Commission on Civil Rights (1967) that
say that things such as the socioeconomic mix of a school really
does matter. It is advantageous to be in a school where some of
your peers are of a somewhat higher socioeconomic class than
yourself. For example, the presence of such students has the effect of raising the expectations of the teachers regarding the performance that can be expected of the students. There are many
studies to show that teacher expectations play an important role
in determining how well students will perform. It would be
nice if teachers in schools with children from low-income house-
holds where a language other than English is just naturally
held high academic expectations. But teachers are human beings, and as with all human beings, many of their attitudes and
the actions that flow from them are unconscious. So, many
times, they will not hold high expectations. Also, when families
with resources are in a school, they tend to demand that the
school system provide adequate resources, and they put some
of their personal resources into the school as well. So having a
range of socioeconomic levels in a school is an asset.

All that aside, I think there can also be clear benefits to a
racially mixed school when careful planning and implementation go into making it succeed. I mentioned earlier the long-
term impacts that have been documented, such as increased job
possibilities and higher education possibilities and opportuni-

ties to develop beneficial networks. But the requirement of careful planning and implementation represents a big caveat. Both good planning and good implementation take lots of time and effort.

From the schools that I have studied, I am convinced that a crucial element in bringing about a successful mixed-race school environment is that teachers conceptualize their role properly. Teachers see themselves first as academics. After all, they teach academic subjects. In our research, we have asked teachers, "Do you teach anything social?" They tend to say something like, "I do tell kids that if they don't come to class, even if they do well on tests, they are not going to pass, because I want to teach them to be responsible." And they mention a great many other social things that they teach. But most of them, in our experience, draw the line at anything that has to do with relations between members of different races. I've had teachers say, "I'm not a social worker." And they are not social workers; I'm not saying they should be. I am saying, however, that in multiracial, multiethnic schools, the price of considering the issue of relations among the student groups to be outside the boundaries of teaching may be that the teacher is less effective than he or she could be.

Let me give you an example. I once saw a class in which the teacher talked about the Romans. In that discussion, he talked extensively about the nobles and the plebeians. At the end, I said, "I thought they had slaves in Rome. Why did you talk about the various classes of Roman people and not mention the slaves?" And the teacher said something like, "Well, this is a desegregated school. I didn't want to raise any racial issues." Here was a teacher who was afraid that talking about the slaves in Rome would raise racial issues that he would be unable to handle. That kind of backing away from the issue is very, very damaging. It means that the teacher can't teach about what kids are concerned about. This is, moreover, a case that is about the truth. Cutting out pieces of social history to avoid sensitive current issues is not being truthful either about the past or about the present. So it is important that teachers in mixed-race schools consider that they can, and really must, have a broad view of teaching, one that includes honest discussion about interpersonal and intergroup relations. They need to be able to teach these things to be effective and to ensure that their teaching remains truthful.

But for teachers to feel that they can teach in this way, they need to be equipped with the skills to handle situations that, admittedly, can be challenging. That gets back to what I said initially. Mixed-race schools can be very good environments for students if that environment has been carefully planned out and if proper preparation has been made to ensure that it will be a positive environment.

Q: *Most school systems that have desegregated have done so under a court-ordered plan. The nature of those orders has varied greatly over the years. Recently, there were two such orders that have been remarkably different from the others. I am talking about the Kansas City case where the judge required equality of outcomes and also the Philadelphia case that also emphasized equality of outcomes rather than such things as physical movement of children from one school to another to achieve racial balance. That is, in both cases, it was the equality of outcomes that was the issue, not the mixing of people or the quality of the classroom or any other of the traditional considerations in desegregation cases. Would you speak to this concept of equality of outcomes?*

A: I do think that striving to achieve equality of outcomes is very important. If you start with the assumption that you can't achieve such an outcome, then you'll never do it. Nevertheless, I do not think that the achievement of equality of outcomes should be a criterion for dismantling a desegregation order. I believe the Kansas City and Philadelphia cases are about setting a criterion for lifting a prior desegregation order. What you would be saying in such a case is that, just at the point where you accomplish something very wonderful and very worthwhile, you would trigger the criterion that would permit the destruction of the very system that brought about the desired result, namely equality of outcome.

So, it seems to me there is an inherent contradiction, or flaw, in seeing the achievement of equal outcomes as the triggering mechanism to indicate that you had "done your duty" and you could now abandon the program that achieved those outcomes. I can begin to see this as a valid triggering mechanism if reaching the objective allows a school system to escape very close supervision so long as it maintains equality of outcomes. If there is that requirement, then it may be a reasonable way to ensure that gains are not lost when court scrutiny is relaxed.

Q: *My real point is that there can be no equality of outcomes. Anyone who thinks so doesn't understand ability. Take teaching the cello as an example. I teach the cello. If you take 10 children and teach each of them, the outcome is not going to be that those 10 kids will know the cello equally well. There is a range of ability. Some people could study the cello for years and not become accomplished cello players. This is no different than saying that not everyone can become an NBA basketball player. So how can there be equality of outcomes?*

A: I agree with you that some people play the cello better than do others. I would never try to compete with Pablo Casals, no matter how good a teacher I had. But that is not the same thing as maintaining that one large group of individuals cannot achieve equal or similar outcomes as are achieved by another large group of individuals. Why? Because, all other things being equal, various abilities are likely to be distributed with about the same frequency within large groups. Each group has its potentially great basketball and cello players and its members who are never going to be cello or basketball players.

It might be well to think of this concept of equality of outcome the way a social scientist would think of it. Remember, I said that if all other things were equal, then the manifestation of various abilities would likely be about the same for both groups. What the social scientist sees is that all other things are not equal. Social scientists know, for example, that social class has a major impact on academic outcomes. The unequal distribution of social class among the groups we are concerned about here is one of the things that makes it difficult to achieve equal academic outcomes. Something must be done to control or compensate for the disparity in income between the groups. Unfortunately, we aren't going to quickly find a way to ensure that all the children in all the various groups come from families with middle incomes. We probably have to look at interim objectives. One such objective might be to ensure that all the children within a social class, regardless of their racial or ethnic background, will perform at a level equal to the majority of members of their social class. If such an objective can be reached, then the next step is to work at raising the performance standard for the members of that social class.

My point is that meeting the goal of having equal outcomes for all ethnic and racial groups is hard to achieve because the conditions that support academic achievement are not bestowed equally on all groups. But its difficulty is not a reason to abandon equality of outcomes as a goal.

Q: *Let's pretend you had to defend your view against somebody like Justice Thomas who might say to you something like the following: "After all these years of desegregation, I am offended by your notion that Blacks can learn only when they are sitting next to Whites." What would you say to that?*

A: I would say that my notion is not that Blacks can learn only when they are sitting next to Whites. That is a misunderstanding for the basis of my positive attitude toward desegregation. I think that there are a number of reasons to be strongly in favor of the policy that don't embody that assumption. For example, although you talked about learning, you didn't talk about what people learn. You will notice that I have talked not just about academic outcomes but also about social outcomes. Now, you could say that I am just talking liberal ideology. But recall that I based some of what I had to say on the SCANS report (Secretary's Commission, 1992), a product of the Bush administration's Department of Labor. That report, you will recall, sets as a priority teaching students the skill of working effectively with people from different backgrounds. Here is a Republican administration identifying learning of the sort that can occur best in desegregated schools as an economic imperative. What is yielded by teaching and learning in a desegregated environment goes well beyond ideology. Republicans and Democrats alike have recognized that to remain strong and prosperous as a people, we all have to learn how to live and work in what is fast becoming a multiracial, multiethnic country. If you go to California, or other places that are at the leading edge of this change, you can see the future for the rest of the country.

The skill called for in the SCANS report is not a simple skill to acquire. You can't learn it from reading a book, but you have to learn it somehow because our society is already diverse and it will become markedly more so. But acquiring that skill, it seems to me, is very difficult if your first exposure to a mixed-race environment doesn't occur until you are 25 or 30 or 40 years old. Desegregation can prepare people early in their lives to live and work comfortably in a social environment where there is racial and ethnic diversity.

My second argument for desegregated schools has to do with resources and the consequences of uneven resource distribution. It is clear that the current majority, the White majority, has more economic resources than do members of the various minority groups. Add to that our understanding that most school financing is very local, relying on property tax or some other form of revenue raising that draws resources from citizens within the township or the county where the schools are located. That form of school finance is unlikely to change radically. Here is where we hit the problem. Cities, or at least inner cities, where a huge number of minority students are educated, are becoming the residences of poor and lower-middle-class minority families. Whites, and I must add, a substantial number of wealthy minority group members, have left the cities or moved to parts of the city that are insulated from multiracial contact. In so doing, they have taken their resources with them.

Put that all together and you have a lot less money being spent on the education of most minority kids than on the education of majority kids or the kids of the few wealthy minority families who also have moved out of the inner cities. I know there are those who say that you can't solve a problem by throwing money at it. Those who make such an argument may not appreciate the contrast between the resources available in suburban schools and those available in many urban schools. They may also not appreciate how often the level of student performance correlates positively with the level of resources in the school. I don't say that money works all the time, but it is frequently helpful. When you have a society that spends considerably more on its majority-group students than it does on its minority-group students, you have a society that is all but certain to stay stratified. That is not a healthy thing for either our economic or our social development. So there are a variety of reasons that desegregated schools make sense for our society. The proposition that Black kids can't learn unless they are next to White kids is not one of them.

Q: *You have referred to social class and resources several times. Could you comment on the Shepard and O'Neil case. It is argued in that case that resources should be allocated according to class rather than race.*

A: I am not familiar with that case. But if I understand your point, you are saying that rather than using methods to redistribute resources so that members of minority groups get more of those resources than they do now, one should resort to methods that redistribute resources from the upper socioeconomic classes to the lower socioeconomic classes more generally. If that is the argument, then I partly agree with it and partly disagree with it.

Here is how I agree with it. I made the argument earlier that if resources are used well, then you can expect that better results will be achieved when more resources are devoted to a given task than when fewer resources are devoted to it. One way of stating the proposition to redistribute resources from upper classes to lower classes is to say, "You really need to pay concerted attention to the education of children who are poor regardless of their color." I have sympathy with that point of view. It is true that we need to ensure that poor kids get a good education. We do need to put more resources into that effort.

But here is how I disagree with the proposition. Race is a crucial factor in our society. It is true that there is considerable overlap between race and socioeconomic level. But that fact sometimes obscures the equally important fact that even an individual who is middle class or upper class and who is African American has certain experiences that a White person of the same class does not experience. It also obscures the fact that there are certain expectations about African Americans that are held by some individuals and that are known by the majority of adults in our society. And those expectations transcend class. They are judgments that are made even before one meets a particular African American for the first time. They are expectations that are not visited on White people. The history of our society and the complexity of our racial attitudes and expectations are too strong to be ignored. Our society has racial inequalities that are not limited by social class. That is why trying to solve educational inequities only by redistributing resources by class is no more than a partial solution. In trying to bring equity to education, we must also pay special attention to race.

•◆••◆••◆•

References

Allport, G. W. (1954). *The nature of prejudice*. Cambridge, MA: Addison-Wesley.

Armor, D. J. (1988). School busing: A time for change. In P. A. Katz & D. A. Taylor (Eds.), *Eliminating racism: Profiles in controversy* (pp. 259-280). New York: Plenum.

Arnez, N. L. (1978). Implementation of desegregation as a discriminatory process. *Journal of Negro Education, 47*, 28-45.

Bell, D. (1980). *Brown* and the interest-convergence dilemma. In D. Bell (Ed.), *Shades of Brown: New perspectives on school desegregation* (pp. 91-106). New York: Teachers College Press.

Blakey, W. A. (1989). *Public school desegregation: Education, equal protection and equality of opportunity*. Norman: University of Oklahoma, Center for Research on Minority Education.

Braddock, J. H., II. (1980). The perpetuation of segregation across levels of education: A behavioral assessment of the contact hypothesis. *Sociology of Education, 53*, 178-186.

Braddock, J. H., II. (1985). School desegregation and Black assimilation. *Journal of Social Issues, 41*(3), 9-22.

Braddock, J. H., II, Crain, R. L., & McPartland, J. M. (1984). A long-term view of school desegregation: Some recent studies of graduates as adults. *Phi Delta Kappan, 66*(4), 259-264.

Braddock, J. H., II, Crain, R. L., McPartland, J. M., & Dawkins, M. P. (1986). Applicant race and job placement decisions: A national survey experiment. *Journal of Sociology and Social Policy, 6*, 3-24.

Braddock, J. H., II, & Dawkins, M. P. (1984). Long-term effects of school desegregation on southern Blacks. *Sociological Spectrum, 4*, 365-381.

Braddock, J. H., II, & McPartland, J. M. (1982). Assessing school desegregation effects: New directions in research. In R. Corwin (Ed.), *Research in sociology of education and socialization* (Vol. 3, pp. 209-282). Greenwich, CT: JAI.

Braddock, J. H., II, & McPartland, J. M. (1987). How minorities continue to be excluded from equal employment opportunities: Research on labor market and institutional barriers. *Journal of Social Issues, 43,* 5-39.

Brown v. Board of Education, Topeka (1954) 347 U. S. 494.

Butler, J. S. (1974). Black educators in Louisiana—A question of survival. *Journal of Negro Education, 43,* 22-24.

Cook T., Armor, D., Crain, R., Miller, N., Stephan, W., Walberg, H., & Wortman, P. (Eds.). (1984). *School desegregation and Black achievement.* Washington, DC: National Institute of Education.

Crain, R. L. (1970). School integration and occupational achievement of Negroes. *American Journal of Sociology, 75,* 593-606.

Crain, R. L. (1984, April). *Desegregated schools and the non-academic side of college survival.* Paper presented at the annual meeting of the American Educational Research Association, New Orleans, LA.

Crain, R. L., & Weisman, C. S. (1972). *Discrimination, personality, and achievement: A survey of northern Blacks.* New York: Seminar Press.

Edelman, M. W. (1973, May). Southern school desegregation, 1954-1973: A judicial-political overview. *Annals of the American Academy of Political and Social Science, 407,* 32-42.

Edmonds, R. R. (1980). Effective education for minority pupils. *Brown* confounded or confirmed? In D. Bell (Ed.), *Shades of* Brown: *New perspectives on school desegregation* (pp. 109-123). New York: Teachers College Press.

Feagin, J. R. (1980). School desegregation: A political-economic perspective. In W. G. Stephan & J. R. Feagin (Eds.), *School desegregation: Past, present, and future* (pp. 25-50). New York: Plenum.

Green, K. (1981, April). *Integration and attainment: Preliminary results from a national longitudinal study of the impact of school desegregation.* Paper presented at the annual meeting of the American Educational Research Association, Los Angeles, CA.

Green, K. (1982). *Integration and educational attainment: A longitudinal study of the effect of integration on Black educational attainment and occupational outcomes.* Unpublished doctoral dissertation, University of California, Los Angeles.

Hamilton, C. V. (1968). Race and education: A search for legitimacy. *Harvard Educational Review, 38,* 669-684.

Haney, J. E. (1978). The effects of the *Brown* decision on Black educators. *Journal of Negro Education, 47,* 88-95.

Hochschild, J. L. (1984). *The new American dilemma.* New Haven, CT: Yale University Press.

Holsendolph, E. (1976, June 20). Figures show integration lag. *New York Times,* p. 24.

Jaynes, G. D., & Williams, R. M., Jr. (1989). *A common destiny: Blacks and American society.* Washington, DC: National Academy Press.

Katz, I. (1964). Review of evidence relating to effects of desegregation on the performance of Negroes. *American Psychologist, 19,* 381-399.

Kluger, R. (1976). *Simple justice: The history of* Brown v. Board of Education *and Black America's struggle for equality.* New York: Knopf.

McPartland, J. M., & Crain, R. L. (1980). Racial discrimination, segregation, and processes of social mobility. In V. T. Covello (Ed.), *Poverty and public policy* (pp. 97-125). Cambridge, MA: Schenkman.

Orfield, G. (1975). How to make desegregation work: The adaptation of schools to their newly-integrated student bodies. *Law and Contemporary Problems, 39,* 314-340.

Orfield, G. (1983). *Public school desegregation in the United States, 1968-1980.* Washington, DC: Joint Center for Political Studies.

Orfield, G., Monfort, F., & Aaron, M. (1989). *Status of school desegregation: 1968-1986.* Alexandria, VA: National School Boards Association.

Pearce, D. (1980). *Breaking down the barriers: New evidence on the impact of metropolitan school desegregation on housing patterns.* Washington, DC: National Institute of Education.

Pearce, D., Crain., R. L., & Farley, R. (1984, April). *Lessons not lost: The effect of school desegregation on the rate of residential desegregation in large center cities.* Paper presented at the annual meeting of the American Educational Research Association, New Orleans, LA.

Pettigrew, T. (1967). Social evaluation theory: Convergences and applications. In D. Levine (Ed.), *Nebraska Symposium on Motivation* (Vol. 15, pp. 241-315). Lincoln: University of Nebraska Press.

Read, F. (1975). Judicial evolution of the law of school integration since *Brown v. Board of Education. Law and Contemporary Problems, 39,* 7-49.

Rosenberg, M., & Simmons, R. (1971). *Black and White self-esteem: The urban school child.* Washington, DC: American Sociological Association.

Rossell, C. H. (1990). *The carrot or the stick for school desegregation policy.* Philadelphia: Temple University Press.

Sampson, W. A., & Williams, B. (1978). School desegregation: The non-traditional sociological perspective. *Journal of Negro Education, 47,* 58-69.

Secretary's Commission on Achieving Necessary Skills (SCANS). (June, 1992). *What work requires of school: Report of the SCANS Commission for America 2000.* Washington, DC: Government Printing Office.

Schofield, J. W. (1982). *Black and White in school: Trust, tension, or tolerance?* New York: Praeger.

Sherif, M., Harvey, O. J., White, B. J., Hood, W. R., & Sherif, C. (1961). *Intergroup cooperation and competition: The Robbers Cave experiment.* Norman, OK: University Book Exchange.

Sizemore, B. A. (1978). Educational research and desegregation: Significance for the Black community. *Journal of Negro Education, 47,* 58-58.

Smith, B. (1965). *They closed their schools: Prince Edward County, VA, 1951-1964.* Chapel Hill: University of North Carolina Press.

Spruill, A. W. (1966). The Negro teacher in the process of desegregation of schools. *Journal of Negro Education, 29,* 80-84.

Tajfel, H. (1970). Experiments in intergroup discrimination. *Scientific American, 223,* 96-102.

Taylor, D. G., Sheatsley, P. B., & Greeley, A. M. (1978). Attitudes toward racial integration. *Scientific American, 238*(6), 42-50.

U.S. Commission on Civil Rights. (1967). *Racial isolation in the public schools.* Washington, DC: Government Printing Office.

Wisdom, J. (1975). Random remarks on the role of social sciences in the judicial decision-making process in school desegregation cases. *Law and Contemporary Problems, 39,* 135-149.

· 2 ·

Ethnicity, Poverty, and Children's Educability

A Developmental Perspective

Diana T. Slaughter-Defoe

ABOUT THIS CHAPTER

Many behavioral scientists try to avoid research outside the laboratory, considering real-life or field settings too messy and uncontrollable to learn anything meaningful. The price for that reticence is often that behaviors that can be elicited in the laboratory with carefully controlled manipulations turn out to be very difficult to reproduce in everyday life. Interventions that show promise under controlled settings are sometimes disappointing when applied to everyday settings, such as the classroom.

NOTE: Portions of this monograph were published in the *American Psychologist*, 1995, 50, 276-286. Copyright © 1995 by the American Psychological Association. Reprinted with permission.

Diana Slaughter-Defoe is a field researcher. She marches in and gets her hands dirty. Maybe her real-life research settings are hard to control, but what she studies is how change is accomplished in the hurly-burly of real life. Her interest is in understanding what causes some children, particularly minority children, to thrive while others are overcome by the obstacles life presents them. What is it that some minority parents do that helps their children excel in school and, ultimately, in life? Can we show parents how to give their children the qualities they need to succeed? Trained as a clinician and a researcher, Slaughter-Defoe dedicates herself to finding interventions that work in practice and to understanding what real people do when they try to cope with the challenges of life.

She does one other hard thing. She studies her subjects longitudinally, that is, over the course of years. It is such research that gives us our deepest insight into human development in the same way that time-lapse photography tells us more about how a plant grows than does a single snapshot. Through her work, we have a glimpse at how a minority child's interaction with his or her parents before and during the school years can aid that child in making the most of formal education.

———————— •◆•————————

◆ Roots of Research on African American Child Development

The Chicago metropolitan area, where I was born and now live and work, is the home of an especially rich tradition in child welfare and child study, as applied to socially and ethnically different groups. Chicago was the home of Jane Addams, a pioneer in the child and family welfare movement. Chicago became the home of Ida B. Wells Barnett, a vigorous Black activist in the antilynching movement, defender of Black families, and crusader for women's rights. Chicago was also the site of the earliest serious scientific attention to the formal education of lower-income children.

Since 1948, when University of Chicago Professor Allison Davis delivered his important address at Harvard University's Graduate School of Education on the topic of "Social-Class Influences Upon Learning," we as a nation have been especially sensitive to the poten-

tially adverse effects of poverty on early school learning and development (Davis, 1948). Even before Davis's explicit discussion of the
sociopsychological processes involved, using the familial lifestyles of
lower-income and Black children as illustrative case examples, social
scientists, such as William Lloyd Warner and colleagues, had deter-
mined that social status differences exist in America that are connected
with educationally significant child behavior, such as intelligence and
achievement-test performance and friendship choices in schools
(Warner & Eells, 1949). Furthermore, 7 years prior to Davis's speech,
in 1941, Chicago was the site of one of the four adolescent studies
commissioned by the American Council on Education. It was titled
Color and Human Nature and was conducted by W. Lloyd Warner and
colleagues in response to the then-emerging Black migrant population
in urban American cities. The four studies, all published between 1939
and 1941 by investigators who had started research careers at the
University of Chicago, appear to be the first major empirical studies
of Black youth in this nation (Davis & Dollard, 1964; Frazier, 1940;
Johnson, 1967; Warner, Junker, & Adams, 1941).

The Legacy of Early Research

My argument in what follows is threefold. The brief background I
have provided supports my first argument, which is that this nation
has long received documentation from its scientific community that
impoverished children and racial/ethnic minority children are disproportionately at risk for educability. Second, the city of Chicago has
been especially active as a total community in bringing this message
to the nation. And third, despite persistent evidence that children's
learning and development are significantly influenced and mediated
by their families, the overwhelming majority of remediation efforts
do not stress active social supports for parent education and family
development. Rather, emphasis has been on the child, the school
curriculum, and educational reform, only incidentally stressing that
successful educational reform is contingent on parental involvement
with the child and the school's curriculum. I want to show you that,
right now, the nation needs demonstration projects and educational
research and evaluation centers that emphasize the study of family
and school relations across the school-aged child's life span. My

experiences while conducting research over the years and my interpretation of my findings occasion this view. That research, of course, grew out of, and builds on, the research tradition and legacy I have just described. In what follows, I will be sharing some of my findings and the conclusions and recommendations I draw from them.

First, I will describe some findings and interpretations from my early research together with the questions that prompted that research. I will discuss four particular field studies. Next, I will discuss my most recent field study, conducted in private schools. Last, I will return to the family policy and educational reform considerations I raised initially.

Do Parent-Child Relations Influence School-Related Performance?

The first study I conducted in relation to this field was conducted as dissertation research and published in *Educational Horizons* in 1969 (Slaughter, 1969). While enrolled as a graduate student in the Committee on Human Development at the University of Chicago, I was a student of Robert D. Hess, who in turn had been a student of Allison Davis whom I mentioned earlier. Both of these scientists had studied how social status differences, indexed simply by such static indicators as occupation, years of education attained, income, and, sometimes, place of residence, contributed, processwise, to sociopsychological outcomes associated with educational performance. In various papers, those authors proposed that families mediated these differences in behavioral interactions with children (Bloom, Davis, & Hess, 1965; Davis, 1960; Hess, 1970; Hess & Shipman, 1965; Hess, Shipman, Brophy, & Bear, 1968). Particular emphasis was placed on verbal interactions and their implications for linguistic development and thought, especially as these factors could contribute to performance on school-related tests. The success of the original research agenda was thought met when parental behaviors were shown to be predictors of 4-year-old Black children's performances in (a) a problem-solving situation with their mothers and (b) independently obtained IQ and subsequent school achievement data on the children. For example, whereas correlations of measures of an individual's social status and IQ were moderate on the average, that is, between .40 and .50, correlations between measures of parenting behaviors and child IQ were obtained as high as .60 to .70. Furthermore, as recently as 1982, Karl White concluded, just as Allison Davis, Robert D. Hess, Benjamin Bloom, and others had a generation before, that the family and home environment are strongly implicated in educational outcomes (Bloom, 1964; White, 1982).

Even in 1969, however, my own emphasis was slightly different—a difference that de-emphasized verbal mediation and instead stressed more global maternal socialization characteristics. Perhaps because of the influence of my clinical training during graduate school, I wanted to know more about the mothers themselves. I hypothesized that mothers who were more "individuating" would have children who were more successful early school achievers. I defined an individuating mother as one who was warm and caring, who knew the personal interests and characteristics of her child and could describe them on request, and who was able to exercise discipline and control over the child without at the same time relinquishing the child's separate individuality. I believed that within a lower-income and Black sample, these maternal characteristics would distinguish the mothers of the more successful preschool children. Success was defined in terms of traditional educational measures: the Stanford-Binet, Metropolitan Reading Readiness Test, preschool teacher evaluations, and the like. I chose as a sample population 90 children, equally divided between males and females, who entered the first 6-week summer Head Start program in 1965. Educational measures were administered during the summer and at the end of the first kindergarten year. At the time of the maternal interview ratings, however, I did not know the educational standing of the children. Results were essentially as I had predicted: The reported maternal behaviors did correlate significantly, though moderately, with the children's educational outcomes.

Since 1969, when this study was published and received an award for its originality, there have been many more sensitive and refined scientific investigations of the correlation between mother-child relations and performance on school-related measures. I am thinking of the particularly rich investigations of Mary Ainsworth (1978), Jean Carew (1980), and Alison Clarke-Stewart (1973). They also concluded that sensitive, informed (i.e., about the child's needs and interests) mothering is beneficial to the early intellectual and social development of infants and toddlers. Indeed, Clarke-Stewart went so far as to specify that the benefits can come regardless of who initiates inter-action. That is, even if infants initiate social interactions, maternal behaviors influence the infant's cognitive development.

Returning to my own work, at least three questions were raised by the original study that were addressed in subsequent work: (a) What would be the longer-term stability and continuity of maternal influence? (b) Were the original results simply reflective of the fact that "smart" mothers have "smart" children, and thus the individuating mother was simply a euphemism for the brighter, smarter mother? (c) What theoretical paradigm would best account for obtained relationships between parental behaviors and school-related child outcomes? It is this latter question that is most centrally related to the topic of the current discussion about the relationship between ethnicity, poverty, and children's educability as these pertain to family and home environment. And I will get to the theory. But, to get to theory, one has to answer the other two questions first. That is what I did in subsequent research.

Relative Influences of Parents and Teachers on a Child's Performance

In two subsequent field studies, first I, and then a dissertation student and I, conducted follow-ups of the children and the mothers who were first studied in my earlier research (Slaughter, 1989; Slaughter & Dombrowski, 1989). The children had attended the Evanston, Illinois, public schools. In the first follow-up, over 50% of the original children and their mothers were interviewed when the children were in Grade 6. Intervening achievement data were obtained from their schools. In the second follow-up, children were interviewed in what should have been their last year of high school. By that time, about one quarter of the original sample remained.

The focus in the first follow-up was on the relative contribution of earlier and current maternally reported behaviors and the history of teacher grades (consistently positive or negative or increasingly positive or negative) to the students' self-perceptions. In the early 1970s, when I received funding from the Social Science Research Council for this research, I argued that the long-term outcomes of schooling would be dependent on student self-perception, both as a learner and as a person. I further argued that the history and pattern of grades received from teachers would influence these self-perceptions. Most important, however, I argued that transition into schools would constitute a discontinuous experience for lower-income and Black children. That is, these children would experience educators as more dominant and authoritative than their parents. Typically, the educators in our study were middle class and White, whereas the parents were lower class and Black, the latter two social parameters commanding less power and fewer resources in U.S. society than the former parameters. Given that disparity, there would be reason to expect that, regardless of early maternal support, once the child was enrolled in school, the opinions of educators would dominate the child's perceptions of academic ability and potential.

My findings in that field study did indeed suggest that (a) these children's self-perceptions about their academic abilities and potential were especially influenced by grades received from teachers, and (b) teachers' grading patterns primarily shaped maternal opinion, which in turn shaped children's views of themselves as far as their academic abilities. I expect the latter finding runs contrary to popular views. Mothers actually adopted the schools' opinions of their children's academic worth. Because mothers are particularly highly valued by their children, these opinions, rightly or wrongly, were in turn adopted by the children. That finding is deserving of much further testing because I think it is a key to improving our understanding of how traditional schools and lower-income, ethnic-minority families typically interact and influence one another. And that interaction has much to tell us about childhood learning and development.

Whereas the mothers of the sixth graders tended to adopt the views of the school about their child's performance, it is important to note that the early preschool behaviors of these same mothers toward their children did not predict the children's achievement standing or self-perceptions at Grade 6. In other words, given the logic of earlier work and scholarship at that time, one would have predicted in that first follow-up study that the home environment in the years 0 to 5 would have consequences for what the children were like in later school ability and performance. The finding in the follow-up study was contrary to that expectation. Instead, the views of the school as mediated by teacher grades on report cards had influenced the parent's opinion of the child's capabilities. This, in turn, was influencing the child's opinion of self. You should keep in mind that this was not a large sample, and thus, the results need replication.

Let me say more about how I reached this view of what was taking place. The children's achievement test performance at Grade 6 in this particular sample was uniformly poor (i.e., below grade level). Their grades, however, were not necessarily perfectly reflective of their achievement test performance, and the children's views of their academic worth varied according to the history of their grades. So their self-evaluations of their abilities as learners were manipulated by the feedback system they received from the school, not their achievement-test results. Nevertheless, in an important sense, the achievement tests were more objective than the grades. I say this because at the time of high school entry, the children are tracked not on the basis of teacher grades but on the basis of their achievement-test performances. Therefore, it would have been important to the children and their parents in that longitudinal sample to receive accurate feedback in the early years about their actual achievement-test performance because it was this performance that governed where they were placed on high school entry.

Perhaps nowhere is the contemporary importance of this line of inquiry better demonstrated than in the research of Doris Entwisle (Alexander & Entwisle, 1988). Her ongoing work began in 1982 in 20 Baltimore public schools. Entwisle and her colleagues have also reported that the transition from preschool into kindergarten may be a life event of considerable significance for lower-income children because of the challenge to their self-perceptions. She goes an important step farther by reporting gender differences in how these self-perceptions of academic ability and potential are formed. That work is demonstrating the rather complex interrelation between home influences and school influences in determining school performance and the child's perception of that performance.

Let me pick up again the thread of my own group's investigation. Our second follow-up took place at our students' 4th year in high school. We focused on factors predictive of these students' educational attainment. My colleague Henry Rubin and I did that by using all of my earlier collected data—maternal variables, grades, achievement-test performances, and child self-perceptions—as potential predictors of future educational aspirations, expectations, and minimal standards for attainment beyond high school (Slaughter-Defoe & Rubin, 1996). Rubin found that, out of all these possible predictors, educational aspirations for the future beyond high school were predicted only by a 7-point rating scale I had administered to the children's preschool teachers nearly 13 years earlier! That rating scale had required the child's preschool teacher to predict the likelihood of the student's success or failure in the school system. It was administered before any substantive academic work had occurred! Aspirations are what a person would like to do. Plans are what a person intends to do. Rubin's observations convinced him and me that economic considerations were more important than earlier background variables in determining our students' immediate post-high school educational plans.

Our longitudinal work following a cohort of children from their years before schooling through the end of high school has led me to conclude that early maternal environment is especially important for poor and minority children's early learning and development. But once these children enter formal schooling, under typical conditions, the parental home environments of these children are themselves affected by the attitudes and opinions of the children's teachers. It appears that teacher attitudes and opinions make an impact on student self-perception through the parents. The student has the primary affective bond with the family rather than with the school. In any event, there is reason to believe that as important as the early mother-child interaction may have been to launching the children, by the time of graduation from high school, more contemporaneous life events play a crucial role in determining the students' future educational plans than do these early interactions. In particular, teacher attitudes and opinions are influential on the children, especially when parents adopt the attitudes and opinions of the teachers.

Can Beneficial Parent-Child Interactions Be Facilitated?

Through all this research, I was unwilling to abandon the concept of maternal individuation. I felt, and still feel, that it really matters whether or not a low-income, Black mother, or any mother for that matter, is a warm, caring, and sensitive informant with respect to her child's personality and development. But finding further support for individuation required further research. That opportunity came when I was able to attempt a replication and verification of the earlier, tentative findings, this time using an appropriate observational play situation as the experimental setting.

As you have gathered from the descriptions so far of my research, I tend to look at behavior over time. This was no exception. The research took the form of a 2.5-year longitudinal study. The research was supported by the National Institute of Child Health and Human Development and the Grant Foundation. In that work, I addressed the question of whether or not the earlier results could be explained by the simple proposition that smart mothers have smart children. That proposition could be contradicted if an intervention would have the effect of changing previously nonindividuating mothers into individuating mothers. At the core of this research was the observational study of mother-child interactions. We had two intervention programs. They were designed for use by toddlers from 18 to 44 months of age and their mothers. Sixty-eight dyads concluded the study. One of the important things their data demonstrated was just what behaviors of individuating mothers were conducive to the infants' success on standard, traditional measures of infant intelligence. What was the nature of their behaviors? These mothers most often interacted with their children in a play session primarily for the purpose of expanding and extending the child's own ongoing play behaviors, whether or not the play included verbalization. So although these mothers may have been warm and supportive and although they may have done some direct teaching with their toddlers, the salient feature of their behavior was that they followed the child's lead and enhanced the child's own efforts. Black mothers categorized as individuating based on their reports of their typical child-rearing practices were more likely to behave in the way I have described than were mothers not categorized as individuating based on their self-reports of typical child-rearing practices.

The correspondence between these individuating behaviors on the mothers' part and the successful performance of their children on standard infant intelligence tests confirmed for me the significance of Black maternal behaviors for their children's early learning and development prior to school entry. But I observed something else as well.

The study was conducted among residents of the Chicago Housing Authority projects. What impressed me greatly were the barriers *and* the potential supports in the neighborhood and community to women rearing children in poverty as single parents. Whether mothers behaved in an individuating way toward their children was partly a function of whether there were social supports that facilitated their behaving in that way. Many of the barriers to such behavior are familiar to us; in fact, the living conditions themselves constitute a major barrier with which the women must cope to successfully maintain their families. That exposure to their social reality, however, convinced me that we must not simply focus on the negative to explain the absence of individuating behaviors. We also need to inform ourselves about potential sources of social support that hold the promise of facilitating mothers to behave in ways that aid the early intellectual development of their children.

One of our two program variables helped bring me to this realization. The manipulation was simple. We created discussion groups in which mothers met weekly to talk about matters of concern to them, whether related to the children or not. That opportunity provided the most consistent positive results across the three housing sites we studied. We did not want prior relationships among these mothers to influence outcomes. The stratified random sampling procedure we used minimized the likelihood that mothers knew one another before their active participation. But by the conclusion of the 2-year program, the women had become sources of social support for one another. For women without extended kin to depend on for help in child rearing, this was especially important. But it was also important to mothers desirous of changing their approach to child rearing. The social support afforded by the discussion group provided the support group that encouraged them in this process. I studied Black mothers, but there is evidence that social support may be a factor in facilitating individuating behaviors in women from many different backgrounds. One piece of evidence in that regard is an article published in *Family Relations* (Powell & Eisenstadt, 1988) in which Douglas Powell reported findings similar to mine with respect to a lower-income White population of mothers.

Here is what I think we have learned from the research I have described so far. First, there is reason to be optimistic that lower-income mothers of infants and toddlers can, and frequently do, engage successfully in what might be identified as bisocialization strategies, that is, interactions with their children that socialize the children to successfully navigate their own communities as well as give them what they need to successfully compete in the early years of traditional schooling. Nevertheless, as I previously indicated, the transition into schools is a significant point of discontinuity for poor, racial and ethnic minority youth. It is a significant transition point in these children's entire care system. As I first argued in 1977, the relationships of child, family, and school to the child's performance have to be reconsidered at that point. After the family is exposed to the attitudes and views of teachers, what the mother conveys to her child through her behaviors may no longer be simply her own child rearing views. There is also an influence of the views of school authorities on the behaviors of mothers toward their children. Fortunately, in recent years, the child development field has made significant contributions to our knowledge base as to how best to provide the necessary positive social supports for those parents who need and want them in matters of child rearing and family development. In fact, in a recent publication, I argued that we are also beginning to learn how to deliver needed services to families in ways that are culturally sensitive and respectful (Slaughter, 1989).

In that article, I outlined some of my own experiences on this issue with lower-income and urban Black parents. For example, I spoke of my experience as a research evaluator, wherein I examined differences and similarities between the way social workers and parents interpret the goals of social work interventions. Using such examinations and other tools developed by my fellow developmental psychologists, we have tools, technologies, for helping to ensure positive, culturally sensitive social support. What disturbs me is that although we have the technical means available to ensure such positive aid to families in need of support, only a few poor families have profited from what we know. I will return to this issue in my concluding remarks, but now I wish to describe another of my field studies. In contrast to the previous studies, it was conducted with middle-income and upper-income Black children in private schools. If taken together with these previous studies of impoverished Black children and their families, the findings begin to give a fuller picture of important general considerations related to race and ethnicity as factors in Black children's educability (Slaughter & Schneider, 1986).

Interactions of Social Class and Parental Influence: A Study of Black, Middle-Class Students in Private Schools

The inspiration for the study came from my interpretation of the results of the earlier described follow-up studies. I wondered how middle-class Black children and their families might differ from impoverished Black families. The academic impetus for this ethnographic field study of middle-school-aged Black children was twofold.

First, as I mentioned earlier, with lower-income racial and ethnic minority families, I found discontinuity between the preschool and in-school development of children. Relative status plays an important role in this discontinuity. The parents of impoverished children typically do not exercise vast social power, and they do not control extensive accumulated resources. Thus, school authorities, who do have social power and have relatively greater resources than do these parents, are likely to influence parental thinking about their children. Moreover, extrafamilial institutions servicing the children and their families are not highly likely to be responsive to their needs and interests. That probability is made the more certain by the inevitable distinctions that exist between the poor, Black families and the more socially and economically dominant school authorities who are also likely to have subcultural histories that differ from those of these families. My families could not ensure that traditional schools would be appropriately responsive to their social and cultural needs. Thus, after the children entered school at age 5 years, it could be expected that the children, influenced by this new environment, would begin to diverge cognitively, socially, and personally from their parents. This is a part of the discontinuity I have referred to since the outset of this discussion. I wondered if Black children whose families were more nearly equal in socioeconomic status to those in authority within their schools might escape this discontinuity. I wondered if, in fact, they might experience continuity in expectations of them between the home and the school and continuity between their preschool and in-school intellectual development.

Second, my earlier research had demonstrated that parents are important influences on the performance of children. That is, for poor families, it was likely to be the case once the children began to attend school that school authorities would influence the perspective of the parents and that the parents, in turn, would influence the children. With that kind of link, one would think that the child's family would be an important component of any model of effective schooling. But the family dimension is decidedly absent from the general literature on effective schools. So I wanted to examine some of the best available real-life examples of quality schooling *for Black children* and extract from them four things: (a) descriptions of Black family-school relations, (b) children's experiences in their classrooms, (c) children's achievements and self-images in such contexts, and (d) the relationship of these factors to reported parental socialization practices.

My colleague Barbara Schneider and I very deliberately chose to focus the research on four desegregated private schools, each with a reputation for academic excellence. These schools offered certain characteristics that I wanted to be present: Each school accepted desegregation as the law of the land. Families who could send their children to private schools were likely to command social power and resources, and that power suggested we would find maximum parental involvement in these schools. In private schools, it seemed likely that it would be relatively easy to describe the philosophy of the school because in these settings, the school's chief administrator is, essentially, also the final authority. Last, because I had originally studied sixth grade public school children, it seemed most appropriate to look at private school students of a similar age. So we chose children in Grades 5 to 8. The schools were all located in Chicago and all had adequate numbers of Black students for our purposes. And important from a practical point of view, there was a willingness at each school to cooperate with us by permitting extensive administrator, teacher, and parent interviews as well as 40 days of classroom observation over the 1983-1984 academic school year. The study yielded rich information that is detailed in our two-volume research report titled, *Newcomers: Blacks in Private Schools* (Slaughter &

Schneider, 1986). This first-of-its-kind study has been available through the ERIC Reproduction Service since 1986. Much more was learned from the study than I can possibly report here. I will, however, highlight the major findings that pertain to the discussion at hand.

First, in these schools, the middle-school-aged Black children performed, on average, at or above grade level in reading comprehension and mathematics computation on standard achievement tests. Furthermore, the children perceived themselves to be academically able. They reported high levels of confidence in their ability to do their school work, and they compared themselves favorably to their White school peers. In fact, the Black children in these private schools perceived themselves to be more socially competent than their peers judged themselves to be. They had very positive self-concepts. On all dimensions of self-concept that we assessed, these Black children's self-evaluations were either similar to, or even higher than, those of peers. On our sociometric measures of peer status, the Black children were as often highly ranked by peers as other children. It should be noted, however, that the Black children received as many peer nominations as other children primarily because of the support they received from own-race peers. It is important to note that our school and classroom observations supported this perspective.

In classrooms, children devoted the majority of time to academic work, and they took considerable pride, regardless of race, in one another's academic accomplishments. Teachers and parents spoke favorably of the children's competencies, both generally and in relation to academic work. Every Black child had at least one or two other-race friends. Although the four educational settings were very different from each other in many ways, they were all philosophically consistent, and in all of them, Black boys in particular appeared to thrive.

But what of Black family-school relations? The concerns of parents differed by school type. Two of the schools were private, elite schools. It was not surprising that in these schools, the major concern of the highly articulate group of Black parents was that the schools be more responsive to the need for the children to experience more in-school opportunities for positive racial and ethnic identity development. Although they supported the educational philosophies of the two elite schools and although they were convinced that children were learning basic skills as well as how to think critically, many of these parents wanted their children's personal-social development to be more actively supported by school administrators and teachers. As real and as genuine as these concerns were to the Black parents, it is my view that they also reflected a conscious effort on their part to increase the comfort of their families and the sphere of their influence in the school as a whole.

In contrast, at the lone Catholic school in our study, which served more of a lower-middle-income Black community, and in which the Black parents tended to be better socially situated than were other parents, these concerns were not expressed. Moreover, these concerns were only infrequently expressed at the fourth school in the study, a private alternative school in which Black children constituted 50% of the pupil population and in which the school's philosophy mandated parental involvement at every level of governance. I am not arguing that the Black parents found no problems with these latter two schools; I am arguing that in these latter two schools, the identified problems less often configured around the central parameters associated with social status in America—class, race, and ethnicity—than was the case at the two elite schools. In other words, when the Black parents complained about the Catholic and the alternative schools, the substance of their complaints did not have directly to do with issues of status and power as mediated by one's social class or racial or ethnic background. Rather than stressing the limited attention to their child's background and culture in the school's curricula, as was the case with complaints at the elite schools, the parents instead focused on the kind of mundane process problems that routinely occur in schools generally. For example, they complained about scheduling problems: "They hold parent meetings at the wrong time of day, when I have to work and cannot get there." In general, they complained about the same kinds of problems that any parent might complain about, regardless of race or ethnic background.

What can be concluded from this study of Black middle-class children? First, Black children, just like all other children, are educable (a) when parents can be influential and actively involved in their children's education; (b) when schools engage in responsible teaching, with an organization and management consistent with their stated educational philosophy; and (c) when parents and schools share mutual respect and this agreed-on educational philosophy. After the preschool years, whether there will be continuity between the home and the school as far as these children's development is concerned depends on how families and schools cooperate in childhood socialization. Even the most positive of early and continuing home environments needs additional supports as children mature. Presently in our society, these supports may be inversely related to poverty and social status. That is, the least support is available where it is needed the most. Though there is a growing body of literature supportive of ethnic and racial differences in cognitive styles, I have found the major educational problems to be more closely identified with the responsiveness of the total school environment to children who are socially and ethnically different. That environment, rather than simply the child's identified psychological characteristics and the responsiveness of a particular teacher or teaching method to those characteristics, determines how the child will fare in the school. Children are not static in their response to school. Quite the contrary. I was amazed at the capacity of the Black children in my study to adapt successfully to a very wide range of educational programs and options. Shirley Brice-Heath (1988) has recently made similar observations about Black children from middle-income families in the southern United States. She has speculated that in contrast to the observed flexibility among the children of these middle-income families, relative inflexibility may characterize many Black children from lower-income communities. Both Brice-Heath (1988) and John Ogbu (1981) emphasize that such children are well adapted to the environments and communities in which they and their families reside, even if they are not so well adapted to the local schools (Ogbu, 1981). It is apparent that we need more information about the contextual and psychological factors that promote resiliency and flexibility in socially vulnerable children. It is apparent that family and home environment are important sources to consider.

I am currently attempting to gather some of that information by initiating yet another follow-up study. It is to be a retrospective study of the then-4-year-old Black children and their mothers who participated in the early 1960s study of parenting and school achievement conducted in Chicago by Robert D. Hess et al. (1968) with 163 Black families from diverse socioeconomic strata. My special focus would be on identification and description of the correlates, if any, in family background, the early parenting environment, and the child's apparent early talents that are most predictive of (a) the child's educational and occupational attainment as an adult and (b) the overall adaptive status of the child's family of procreation, where relevant. Hess has become interested in the project. We have discussed beginning by using the available early data to make our best scientifically based guesses about what is important to the social status and well-being of these children and their families. Then, we will set about locating the families and finding out what in fact has turned out to be important for them in terms of social status and well-being. So we plan to see how good a predictor the early data were of what would be important for these children and their families. I am especially enthusiastic about the possibilities of this research effort because the sample was originally socially heterogeneous. Thus, the early parenting and family data collected were particularly rich and reliable. These data should provide a good base for examining the relationship between early and later life events and individual and familial life course outcomes. Furthermore, the participating Black children have among their number both those who attended private schools and those who attended public schools. Already, persons have contacted me at Northwestern University from as far away as Oklahoma expressing a desire to participate in this follow-up!

Implications for Educational Reform: Don't Forget Family and Home Environment

I thank my mentors for the fact that I began my research career with a healthy respect for the importance of the family and home environment in children's educability. Now, with several decades of research under my belt, I have come to appreciate how complex the influence of family and home is on the development of children and on the development of the institutions into which these children are placed for their education. If we are going to educate poor and ethnic minority children well, I believe we need to achieve a much better understanding than we have now of how the ethnicity and social status of the family influence the children's social and psychological development. Because we have virtually no normative data on these children, it should be no surprise that we have problems making good decisions about curriculum and instruction for these children. These are problems that no amount of ideology can solve in the absence of high-quality empirical data.

I am aware of the many reasons families have not been given priority in contemporary considerations of educational reform. Many fear that educators use children's families to avoid their own accountability for educational service delivery. Others fear that children's learning potentials are too often stereotyped by educators who prefer to expect less of children from certain family backgrounds. Both of these positions were argued by Kenneth B. Clark (1965) in *Dark Ghetto* some years ago. Still others feel that little positive help can be forthcoming to educators from families of children who are embattled by poverty and unemployment, crime-ridden neighborhoods, and deteriorating societal and social values. Many appear to believe that meeting the economic and social needs of families in other areas (e.g., housing, health care, child care) will automatically translate into education-related benefits for children. Last, many continue to be concerned that any governmentally supported intervention into family life, even on behalf of children, could endanger the rights of all U.S. families to form families and rear children in those families as they see fit. Each position leads, logically and unfortunately, to diminution of attention to child-parent and family relations in the context of educational reform. Given the changing nature of U.S. families, however, all U.S. children could benefit from carefully disseminated findings to educational institutions on educability issues associated with children who are from impoverished families and, in particular, those children from impoverished families who have also been identified as racial or ethnic minority children in our society: American Indians, Asian Americans, Black Americans, and Hispanic Americans.

Neither a child's poverty nor ethnicity, as far as my research indicates, needs to be a barrier to educability. However, I think what is required to overcome barriers and provide social supports to impoverished and ethnic minority children and families is respect and acknowledgment of their parents' crucial role in the educational process. Parents are important because of the children's affective ties to them, because they are the children's most enduring teachers, and because our democracy recognizes the parent as that person legally responsible for the child's welfare. Conversely, I believe it is the society's responsibility to ensure that those who do parent have access to the best available and most useful information and assistance—the needed resources to provide a quality home environment.

————•◆•————•◆•————•◆•————

Q: *You spoke of the importance of the transition from home to school. What about the transition to day care? Is it important? If so, how much?*

A: In our particular research, it was not a factor. I would count the years 0 to 5 as a separate kind of experience from the rest of childhood development, whether those years include day care or not. For one thing, the adult-child ratio is a lot better than it is in succeeding years of schooling. My cousin, for example, is currently teaching in a Chicago public school. The school in which he teaches is quite ordinary. It is not part of a demonstration program, and so forth. He is teaching 44 youngsters in the third grade. He told me that 10 of them read at a second grade level; everyone else reads at an even lower level! This is not an all-Black school but one that has Hispanics, Blacks, and a number of other groups. That is a very different experience than a day care setting where a ratio of 1 adult to 17 children is considered optimal. In a typical public school situation, the ratio of adults to children is quite different.

Robert Dreeben (1968), a sociologist, has addressed the difference between formal schooling and the informal home environment experience very nicely. He points out that aside from these adult-child ratios, there is a certain expectation between the teacher and the child in the typical first grade classroom. It is quite different from home in the early years. At school, there is a more formal relationship with adults in authority. The child has to share with same-age peers. The organization and management of formal school provide a different type of psychological experience for children than the individuated, close, particularized experience within most familial home environments.

Q: *We are beginning to witness in America a new class of children, the homeless. Have you done any studies, and if not, do you care to share your concerns about that?*

A: I am very glad, Congressman, you mentioned that because we talked earlier during lunch about the homeless. When I began these longitudinal studies years ago, we were not seeing what we are now seeing in our cities. These people were quite poor, but they had shelter. So we did not have a phenomenon such as we have seen in the last few years—families who are sending their children to schools from a shelter for the homeless. The most rapidly increasing group, as far as I can learn, in the overall impoverished community, is single women who have suddenly found themselves homeless and who also have children. What I have been able to learn is that other children in the schools are aware that these children do come from shelters, and there is a certain amount of stigmatizing that is occurring. The homeless children are at risk partly because of stigmatization. We have next to no information on this topic, and I think it is really important that we do appreciate and understand that, right now, there are different degrees of poverty.

Probably, the most impoverished situation includes children whose families do not have a stable physical home environment or shelter. The children might be living in cars or moving from shelter to shelter, as they do in the city of Chicago. Let me just state, without having specifically collected information on this population, that the child development literature would simply predict extreme psychological deprivation in such a situation. Not being able to have even a stable physical environment while shaping one's own early identity and cognitive development would certainly not be conducive to having any successful experiences in school. But what we need is more positive information on this topic—such as who are the children and families able to take this most destitute of experiences and make something of it for themselves. Then, we can learn about how to support those potential resiliencies.

Q: *Along those same lines, one group that really sticks in my mind is the Vietnamese students who live in extremely poor situations. In northern Virginia, there are several high school valedictorians whose parents came over here with nothing. Has there been any study done to show what kind of support groups those mothers might have that might be different from other lower-income groups?*

A: You have raised some really good points because part of what gets studied depends on who is around. We need to start "perking up" the research because, no pun intended, the complexion of Head Start has changed dramatically in the last 20 or so years! For example, in a review of the literature on the social and pretend play of ethnic and racial minority children that I conducted with a colleague, Joseph Dombrowski (Slaughter & Dombrowski, 1989), only one anecdotal study about the play of Vietnamese children in preschools was found. There may be studies in the pipeline of which I am presently unaware, but I think we presently need more scholars interested in doing research in this area.

Also, by way of anecdote, many of these families are not as unstable from an economic standpoint as you might expect, because they are not in the category of welfare recipients. They have refugee status, and what that means concretely, as far as I have been able to determine, is that people prefer to rent to them because their income is perceived by potential landlords, including minority landlords, as more stable. A few months ago, I spent some time in California because my father was ill. There is a large Laotian and Cambodian community that has come to the West Coast, and both the Hispanic and Black populations were finding themselves displaced in terms of housing, and they were being displaced even by the Black landlords. The perception was that the economic stability of these new groups was a little bit better because of the refugee status they had than was the stability of the Hispanics and Blacks. This is what I meant when I said to Congressman Dymally that it does not

seem like much to a person like you or me, but these little grada-
tions or degrees of poverty can sometimes make a big difference
between a child having a relatively secure and safe place to live
versus moving from one homeless shelter to another.

Q: *I work with Head Start. My question is twofold. First, Head Start
serves only 20% of all eligible children. The reason everyone agrees
Head Start is so successful, and indeed it is a very bipartisan program,
is because the parents are involved on all levels, even developing curricula for their children. My concern is for the 80% of poor children who
are not being served. How could we motivate the parents? What is the
individual motivational aspect, and how can we get that to filter down
to the child? My second question has to do with the approximately
26% of children in Head Start right now who are by and large bilingual and, therefore, bicultural—mostly Hispanic (3% are Asian) but
also American Indians, Haitian, and so forth. In my short experience,
the language has been so important in the retention because it focuses
around the home environment. What research can you offer to us as far
as the importance of maintaining not only the primary language but
the whole cultural identity of the child?*

A: On your first question, it is not simply a question of individual
motivation in Head Start as far as we have been able to determine. There is a disproportionately low participation rate
among Whites who are eligible for Head Start. In my opinion,
that is a group to concentrate on. We need to know why they
do not participate in this program in proportion to their representation in this entire society. We should then try, based on
those findings, to increase their participation rates. I would
theorize that one of the reasons Head Start has remained at
level funding and has not been able to take on some of the issues that it could, is in part that it has not addressed this issue.

At Northwestern University, we teach students from a great
variety of backgrounds, and we have a number of students who
are from White, rural communities. I would say there is a feeling of embarrassment and shame about their impoverished con-
dition, maybe sometimes carried to the extreme. To participate
in a program such as Head Start would be perceived by some

Whites as receiving a handout. This would be my explanation for the lower rates of participation among poor White families. I think until that barrier is overcome, at least for a significant portion of that group, you will have what I would consider a problem in that Head Start is not able to extend its net to include more eligible children. I am not simply saying that the majority of the eligible children are poor Whites; what I am saying is that until proportionate numbers of that group are active in Head Start, it is not likely we will be able to improve the levels of funding received by Head Start. One of the main parameters tied to a social program of this type has to do with the family's attitude toward participation in the program itself, which, to some extent, is ethnicity-related and regulated. I think I would tackle that one before focusing on individual motivation.

On the question of bilingualism, I do not know how to answer that; I will just be quite honest with you. That is an extremely complex question. I think, however, there are people who have done some excellent research on the relationship between language and identity development, although there is not nearly enough research. I think Head Start has had a good measure of success in comparison to the lack of success in elementary and secondary schools in involving persons from all of these diverse backgrounds. Maybe the National Education Association and the other groups could learn something from you. I think that professionals at the early-childhood level should be working more closely with professionals in elementary and secondary education so the latter can draw on this expertise. Frankly, the early-childhood professionals have a much stronger track record of success in working out these problems. Some colleagues and I discovered in a recent overview of the Head Start literature on bilingualism that there are at least four or five different types of multicultural demonstration programs currently operating. In other words, Head Start has pilot programs that show where one can go to learn how to work with pre-school-aged children who are linguistically different. I do not think that comparable programs really exist at the elementary and secondary level, and we could probably learn from Head Start. But we will not be able to take advantage of the wisdom of those pilot programs as long as we treat them as discrete educational programs rather than structured experiences designed to benefit the psychological development of children.

Q: *Given what you say about the importance of parents to children's success in school, to what extent are extended-family relationships useful?*

A: I did not tell you about all of my research because it did not pertain directly to the subject of my talk, but I became really interested in that very question and decided to test it in an extreme situation. We were studying psychosocial factors affecting Black children with sickle-cell disease. I figured if the idea or concept of the extended family had any scientific utility, we ought to see it with children who were chronically ill. What, indeed, did a parent do in that situation, and what role would the extended family play? Basically, we worked with 34 families of children enrolled at either Children's Memorial or the University of Illinois hospitals in Chicago, with financial support from the March of Dimes Foundation (Slaughter & Dilworth-Anderson, 1990).

A colleague, Peggye Dilworth-Anderson, and I identified children 8 to 11 years of age who had been diagnosed as having sickle-cell disease. (This is a genetically transmitted disease that can result in unpredictable periodic intervals of severe pain in the joints and limbs because blood does not flow normally and smoothly.) We asked, what kinds of social supports do the mothers, always the primary caregivers in our study, of these children get and from whom? They were asked, "Next to yourself, who is the person to whom you most look to support you in the care of your child?" Most often, they would say the children's father, if they did not report their own mother. When we asked them what kind of support they looked for, they had several options. The one they usually mentioned was that they looked for affection and intangible sources of support—to feel someone is on their side who is not always giving them advice and telling them what to do, someone who is in their corner no matter what. They could depend on that person to stand with them.

We discovered that the father was typically the only person who was turned to for this type of support. He was the mother's alter ego. If she were not around to help the child when he or she was in severe pain, the father would help. The father would basically do what the mother did. On the other hand, the maternal grandmother, maternal aunt, or extended family members were more likely to provide backup—"I will stay home with the other children while you take the child to the hospital," or, "I will prepare the meals while you are at the hospital." It was only the fathers who would do exactly what the mothers would do—that is, stroke the child's arm so the pain would go away, take the child to the hospital, and so forth. Maybe that is why mothers did not perceive that paternal help as tangible support.

They categorized that as affection, whereas when they talked about the support they received from their mothers and sisters, for example, they discussed it in terms of more tangible resources and supports. About 50% of the sample received help from fathers, whether or not they were present in the home. Another 25% received help from maternal kin. And another 25% said they had no one they could turn to at all. This was especially true of the more impoverished families; some of these maternal caregivers could not get help. There are people who simply have no one, or who perceive that they have no one, they can trust to help them. I suspect the same is true of childhood academic achievement socialization in Black communities.

•◆••◆••◆•

References

Ainsworth, M. (1978). *Patterns of attachment*. Hillsdale, NJ: Erlbaum.

Alexander, K., & Entwisle, D. (1988). Achievement in the first 2 years of school: Patterns and processes. *Monographs of the Society for Research in Child Development, 38* (6-7, Serial No. 218).

Bloom, B. (1964). *Stability and change in human characteristics*. New York: John Wiley.

Bloom, B., Davis, A., & Hess, R. D. (1965). *Compensatory education for cultural deprivation*. New York: Holt, Rinehart & Winston.

Brice-Heath, S. (1988). Language socialization. In W. Damon (Series Ed.) and D. Slaughter-Defoe (Vol. Ed.), *Black children and poverty: A developmental perspective* (New Directions for Child Development, Vol. 42; pp. 29-42). San Francisco: Jossey-Bass.

Carew, J. (1980). Experience and the development of intelligence in young children. *Monographs of the Society for Research in Child Development, 45* (1-2, Serial No. 183).

Clark, K. B. (1965). *Dark ghetto: Dilemmas of social power.* New York: Harper & Row.

Clarke-Stewart, K. A. (1973). Interactions between mothers and their young children: Characteristics and consequences. *Monographs of the Society for Research in Child Development, 38* (6-7, Serial No. 153).

Davis, A. (1948). *Social class influences upon learning.* Cambridge, MA: Harvard University Press. (Also known as The Inglis Lecture, 1948, invited by Harvard, and given when Davis was a professor at the University of Chicago.)

Davis, A. (1960). *Psychology of the child of the middle class.* Pittsburgh: University of Pittsburgh Press.

Davis, A., & Dollard, J. (1964). *Children of bondage.* New York: Harper & Row. (Original work published 1940)

Dreeben, R. (1968). *On what is learned in school.* Reading, MA: Addison-Wesley.

Frazier, E. F. (1940). *Negro youth at the crossways: Their personality development in the middle states.* Washington, DC: American Council on Education.

Hess, R. D. (1970). Social class and ethnic influences on socialization. In P. Mussen (Ed.), *Carmichael's manual on child psychology* (Vol. 2, pp. 457-558). New York: John Wiley.

Hess, R. D., & Shipman, V. C. (1965). Early experience and the socialization of cognitive modes in children. *Child Development, 34,* 869-886.

Hess, R. D., Shipman, V. C., Brophy, J., & Bear, R. (1968). *Cognitive environments of urban preschool Negro children* (Vols. 1 & 2). Report to the Children's Bureau, Social Security Administration, U.S. Department of Health, Education and Welfare, Washington, DC.

Johnson, C. (1967). *Growing up in the Black belt.* New York: Schocken. (Original work published 1941)

Ogbu, J. (1981). Origins of human competence: A cultural-ecological perspective. *Child Development, 52*(1), 413-429.

Powell, D., & Eisenstadt, J. (1988). Informal and formal conversations in parent discussion groups: An observational study. *Family Relations, 37,* 166-170.

Slaughter, D. (1969, Fall). Maternal antecedents of the academic achievement of Afro-American Head Start children. *Educational Horizons, 48,* 24-48.

Slaughter, D. (1989). Programs for racially and ethnically diverse American families: Some critical issues. In H. Weiss & F. Jacobs (Eds.), *Evaluating family programs* (pp. 461-467). Hawthorne, NY: Aldine.

Slaughter, D., & Dilworth-Anderson, P. (1990). Sickle cell anemia, child competence, and extended family life. In H. Cheatham & J. Stewart (Eds.), *Black families: Interdisciplinary perspectives* (pp. 131-148). New Brunswick, NJ: Transaction.

Slaughter, D., & Dombrowski, J. (1989). Cultural continuities and discontinuities: Impact on social and pretend play. In M. Bloch & A. Pellegrini (Eds.), *The ecological context of children's play* (pp. 282-310). Norwood: Ablex.

Slaughter, D., & Schneider, B. (1986). *Newcomers: Blacks in private schools* (Vols. 1 & 2; Report No. NIE-G-82-0040, ERIC Document Reproduction Service Nos. ED 274 768 and ED 274 769). Evanston, IL: Northwestern University School of Education and Social Policy.

Slaughter-Defoe, D., & Rubin, H. (1996, May). *Factors influencing the educational goals of low-income African American students: Implications for early childhood programs and parental involvement*. An unpublished paper for the APA Task Force on Poverty. (Available from Diana T. Slaughter-Defoe, Human Development and Social Policy Program, School of Education and Social Policy, Northwestern University, 2115 N. Campus Drive, Evanston, IL, 60208.)

Warner, W. L., & Eells, K. (1949). *Social class in America*. Chicago: Science Research Associates.

Warner, W. L., Junker, B., & Adams, W. (1941). *Color and human nature*. Washington, DC: American Council on Education.

White, K. R. (1982, May). The relation between socioeconomic status and academic achievement. *Psychological Bulletin, 91*(3), 461-481.

·3·

User-Friendly Science and Mathematics

Can it Interest Girls and Minorities in Breaking Through the Middle School Wall?

Jacquelynne Eccles

ABOUT THIS CHAPTER

The middle school years are a critical make-or-break point for girls and minority students. Experiences they have, and decisions they make then, can effectively determine the options they will be prepared to pursue during the remainder of their education and the career choices that will be realistic for them. Given those consequences, it is essential for scientists to understand what exactly is going on in these middle school years that causes so many girls and minority students to behave in ways that will severely limit the choices they will have in life. It is essential to understand because that is the first step in altering environments so as to assure the middle school years expand, not limit, opportunity.

Like the other researchers in this volume, Jacquelynne Eccles is an activist. Not content simply to understand, she wishes to cause positive social change. Her research points the way to changing middle schools so that they will nurture the aspirations of all children, particularly those most at risk during early adolescence. Beyond her research, Dr. Eccles has also given her time to connecting science with policy. Not only has she come to Washington to explain her findings to lawmakers. She has also chaired the National Science Foundation's (NSF) Committee on Equal Opportunity in Science, Engineering and Technology, a congressionally mandated body that helps the NSF create and monitor programs that promote the entry of women, minorities, and those with physical disabilities into science and engineering and that reports to Congress on the progress made by the Foundation. She has also chaired the Advisory Committee of the NSF's Directorate for Social, Behavioral, and Economic Sciences, the NSF division that supports most of the behavioral and social science research in the country, including much of the research relevant to girls and members of minority groups.

———————•◆•———————

I'd like to begin this discussion with a joke. That is often a good ice breaker. But I can't. The issues we have to discuss are too serious. They are so serious that the American Association for the Advancement of Science (AAAS) is calling for a radical reform in science and math education from preschool through the university. Their report on the state of science education in the United States (Rutherford & Ahlgren, 1990) makes clear that many U.S. citizens, even those who are otherwise well educated, have little understanding of science or how it affects their standards of living nor do they possess the intellectual skills to act effectively on scientific matters that they encounter in their personal, professional, and civic experiences. The report also emphasizes how especially critical it is that we recruit more women and minorities into science-related careers and into the teaching of science: With changing demographics in the next 20 years, and I won't bore you with all those statistics, it is very clear that we will not be able to meet our resource needs if we continue to rely primarily on the White male population, our source in the past for scientists. In fact, the situation is serious enough that unless more young women and minorities choose to concentrate in the natural sciences, jobs calling for specialized preparation may go unfilled.

The late Betty Vetter, who was a deeply valued member of the Scientific Manpower Commission in Washington, D.C., was among the strongest advocates of that same position. The data she produced has been extremely valuable to those in my field of research. She prepared numerous reports showing that if we project from right now and look at what is likely to happen over the next 20 or 30 years, we are facing a very serious problem in terms of lack of person power. And the only way we will solve that problem will be by recruiting minorities and women into science and maintaining them in such careers. We need to do that in addition to continuing to tap the white male talent pool.

What I find most disturbing about the AAAS report is that it is not "new news"—that is, we've known this for quite a while. I went to a talk that Vetter gave 10 years ago; she laid out the problem quite succinctly clear back then. And several past presidents of AAAS have chosen to focus their presidential addresses on this particular issue. I became interested in the question of why women and minorities do not choose to go on in math and science when I responded to a Request for Proposals on this topic from the National Institute on Education (NIE), which no longer exists. NIE targeted money to develop a body of research on that topic, which led to a large number of researchers becoming interested in it. And that was in 1977! The problem persists, however: Some of Vetter's last statistics show the number of women entering engineering peaked in 1985 at 18%; currently, it's back to 14% (Vetter, 1989). And, as most of you know, the number of college-aged students has declined over the last 10 to 15 years. So the pool from which we are going to draw our scientists, mathematicians, and engineers continues to shrink.

In my discussion, I will make five major points:

1. We have a very serious problem with the level of training U.S. students receive in math and science, and it is affecting the supply of adequately trained workers at all levels of proficiency. It is easy to focus on the few numbers who are entering bachelor's degree programs in math or science, but the issue is much more serious than that. The issue is that a very, very small proportion of our students are leaving secondary school with training in math and science adequate enough even to operate in the workforce, much less to specialize in those fields.

2. This problem is especially marked for minorities and for females, although for slightly different reasons.

3. For minorities, in particular, the problem is symptomatic of an even larger problem of inadequate education and high dropout rates. Their problem is not just in math and sciences but across the board.

4. The high dropout rate among minorities as well as the low involvement of women and minorities in math and science result in part from the educational climate and organizational structure prevalent in our junior high schools—in particular, low teacher sense of efficacy, person-unfriendly instructional practices in the math and science courses, ability level tracking, large size and bureaucratic organization, and inadequate adult-child personal contact.

5. Changes in these aspects of the middle-grade educational climate and organizational structure can ameliorate declines in both general school motivation and interest in math and science.

Before addressing these issues, let me give you (a) some background on how I became interested in this particular research problem and on why I have centered my research attention on middle schools, and (b) let me give you a brief picture of how serious our math and science problem is in the United States, particularly for women and minorities.

I was initially interested in the general question of sex differences in career choice. My interest began in college when I looked around (this was in the late 1970s) and realized there were four women in our graduate program in psychology—and psychology is a field that attracts women! I began to wonder what was different about the four of us. Why were we there? Why were none of the women with whom I had gone to high school there?

Then I learned that the NIE had issued a request for proposals to look at why females weren't going on in math and science. I thought this was an excellent opportunity to try to translate my personal question into a research question. So I began to look at that question, focusing specifically on junior and senior high school.

The more I got into that work, the clearer it became that "something" was going on at the *junior* high school level. I saw that females were, indeed, less likely than males to go on in math and the sciences. But even more interesting was a fundamental developmental question: Why were very few people *in general* going on in math and science? The dropout rate was exceedingly large. Something was happening during junior high school that was affecting both males and females. Keep in mind that I was looking at white, middle-class school districts, not inner-city school districts suffering from major, horrendous problems. I saw that kids were "turning off" to math and science during this period of time—all kids, kids who were doing well and kids who were doing poorly. This made me very interested in what might be going on in junior high school. That is why the work I have done since has looked at this transition. So that's how I became interested in this problem and involved in the Carnegie report on education in the middle grades as well (Task Force, 1989)!

How Serious Is the Problem?

From data produced by Vetter (Task Force, 1988) let me illustrate the declining interest of students in the United States in studying math, science, and engineering. If we start with 7 million kids who are moving through the educational system, what can we predict if they follow the path that currently exists? By seventh grade, only 11% of the original group of 7 million express an interest in those fields. That means we've lost 89% of the kids by junior high school! By high school, that drops to 8%; by college entrance, 5%. The number who actually get B.S. degrees in math, science and engineering is only 3%, and only 1% go on to graduate programs in those fields. At the doctorate level,

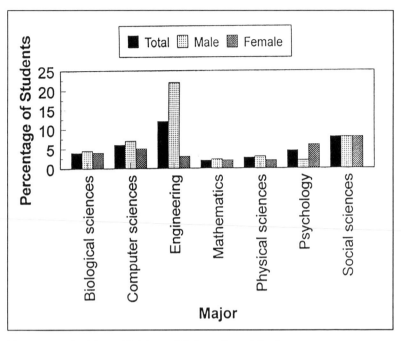

Figure 3.1. Anticipated Majors of College-Bound Seniors
SOURCE: Adapted from Vetter & Babco (1987).

we're down to 0.15% of the original population. So that is the nature of the problem we're talking about. And the percentages are far less if we consider only minorities or women (or both)!

In 1982, the average high school graduate had taken 2.2 years of science and 2.7 years of math in the last 4 years of secondary school education. What this means is that, by tenth grade, most kids are finished with math and science. The situation, again, is even worse for minorities and women, especially with regard to advanced-level math and physical sciences. For example, on the average, only about 10% to 15% take introductory physics in high school. And, indeed, only 5% of Hispanics have had some exposure to physics in high school.

Figure 3.1, from Vetter's data (Vetter, B. M., 1981), illustrates the sex differences in the choices of the approximately 32% of college-bound seniors whose first choice was to major in math, science, or engineering.

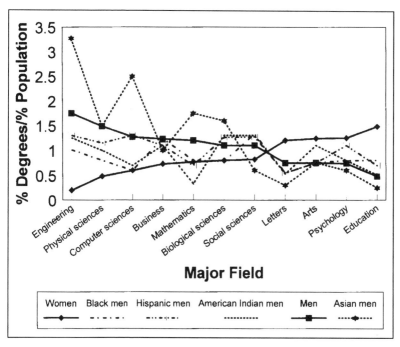

Figure 3.2. Majors for Bachelor of Arts Degrees by Gender and Ethnic Group of the Males
SOURCE: Chipman and Thomas (1984).

Figures 3.2 and 3.3 are from the work of Chipman and Thomas (1984). The figures show the propensity to select major fields at the bachelor's level, showing the distribution of degrees in different areas by their proportion in the population—for men and women as well as for American Indian, Black, Hispanic and, Asian men (Figure 3.2) and women (Figure 3.3). If the proportion of degrees for a group were equal to its proportion in the undergraduate population, the line would be at 1.0.

But as I said, I think the problem is much more serious. The problem isn't just the declining number of kids who are going on to seek advanced training in math and science. And the problem isn't just that even fewer women and minorities are going on to seek advanced training in math and science. Nor is the problem only the shortage of scientific person power this nation faces as a result of the first two

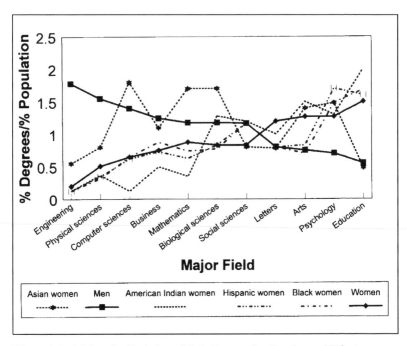

Figure 3.3. Majors for Bachelor of Arts Degrees by Gender and Ethnic Group of the Females
SOURCE: Chipman and Thomas (1984).

problems. We have a more fundamental problem. Kids are not getting very good math and science training across the board:

- The latest round of National Assessment of Educational Progress (NAEP) tests, for example, suggests that kids today are still performing below the level that U.S. kids were performing in math and the sciences in the mid-1970s, and they are below all other industrialized countries.

- Blacks and Hispanics, by age 17 years, are testing 4 years behind their White peers in the sciences, although there has been an increment in their relative position.

- At age 17 years, less than one half of the kids in the United States have enough math knowledge as measured by the NAEP to take a job requiring technical skills or to take a job requiring them to learn technical skills on the job. Only 7% have learned enough math and science to take a basic-level course in science at college.

♦ In addition, according to the latest data, the gap between men and women in knowledge of math and science has more than doubled since 1970. And this gap is just as large among men and women taking the highest levels of math and science as it is for those taking lower levels.

♦ Nearly one half of young adults are unable to do well on tasks of even moderate complexity, such as balancing a checkbook or using a map.

♦ If we look at trends in SAT scores, we find a fairly consistent pattern across the years from 1976 to 1985: White students perform better than all other groups on the verbal scores, and Asian and White students perform better than all other groups on the math scores. None of our interventions over this period seems to have changed these inequities in performance.

♦ In the Hispanic population across the country, by age 13, close to 50% are already behind in school by at least 1 year.

That last point is an important one because falling behind in school is one of the best predictors of subsequent dropout. As soon as kids start to fall behind, especially in the junior high school years, they appear to be on a track that leads many of them to dropping out. Incidentally, dropout statistics are interesting because they do not make clear whether someone is a dropout for his or her entire life. At what point do you classify a person permanently as a dropout? For Hispanic groups between the ages of 18 and 21 years, 35% nationwide are not in secondary school and are not on a GED track toward graduating from high school. A proportion of these dropouts do eventually go back. The number is lower for Blacks and Hispanics than for Whites. It is much lower for females than for males.

Being a dropout increases the odds of being unemployed or if employed, that the employment is intermittent or at a job that is marginal or below the level of one's skills. The Carnegie Council's *Turning Points* summarizes the costs of school dropouts at national and personal levels (Task Force, 1989):

- ◆ Each year's class of dropouts, over their lifetime, will cost the nation about $260 billion in lost earnings and foregone taxes.
- ◆ Each added year of secondary education reduces the probability of public welfare dependency in adulthood by 35%.
- ◆ In a lifetime, a male high school dropout will earn $260,000 less than a high school graduate and contribute $78,000 less in taxes. A female who does not finish high school will earn $200,000 less and contribute $60,000 less in taxes.
- ◆ Unemployment rates for high school dropouts are more than twice those of high school graduates. Between 1973 and 1986, young people who did not finish high school suffered a 42% drop in annual earnings in constant 1986 dollars.

Why is this happening? Why are we seeing these low levels of achievement, these high rates of dropout, and this lack of involvement in science and education?

Let me step back and talk about what I think is going on in the junior high and why I'm looking at that period in particular as being very important. As I said, we began doing our work looking at sex differences in interest in math and science. That was the primary question of interest to us.

What we did was to go out and gather surveys and sit in math and science classrooms in junior and senior high schools all over southeastern Michigan. At this point, I have assessed more than 3,000 kids, and my colleagues and I have looked at hundreds of hours of classroom instruction. We looked at the classrooms in a variety of ways. We used what we call a high-inference methodology, where we essentially sat in the back of the classroom for a week and formed an impression about what was going on. We also used low-inference techniques, where we looked at the teacher's interaction with every child in the classroom and reported exactly what went on, to see whether boys and girls were being treated differently in the math and science classrooms.

As I said, these are mainly White, middle-class students from 15 different school districts in southeastern Michigan. They come from families of low-middle to middle socioeconomic status. We didn't have a lot of minorities; we didn't go into the inner-city Detroit

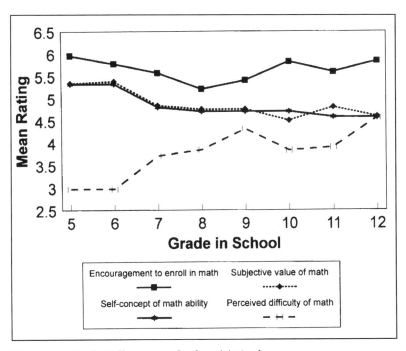

Figure 3.4. Grade Differences in Students' Attitudes
SOURCE: Adapted from Midgely, Feldlaufer, and Eccles (1989b).

schools. We tried to pick schools without any major problems. These are kids who are headed toward college and headed toward being able to take advanced math. They have not had any difficulty. At the start of our studies, they had not been tracked down or tracked out of math classrooms. We asked them (a) how difficult they thought math was, (b) how good they thought they were in math, (c) how much they liked math and felt it was useful for their long-range goals (the subjective value of math), and (d) their perceived encouragement to enroll in advanced math. We asked them these same questions about English, and in English, we got no developmental trends: The kids remained positive toward English throughout secondary school. They felt good about their English abilities, and they didn't find English especially difficult. But in math, as you can see in Figure 3.4, we found a very different pattern. And again, what's important about this is that these kids are doing well in math.

As you can see, what we found is they get increasingly negative about math—they begin to see math as more difficult, they become less confident about their abilities, and so forth. Also, you'll note the dramatic break in the curves between sixth and seventh grades. That is the point at which you see the biggest change on all four curves. This was the first hint we had that something was going on in the junior high school. We have now replicated this in 12 different school districts. The pattern follows the same trend across school districts.

So the transition to junior high school becomes the critical point. We weren't initially interested in studying this transition. In fact, it never even occurred to us to study it! We used the junior high for sex difference reasons. We knew we would see these differences emerging at puberty—especially among the females who sprout breasts, start menstruating, get interested in boys, and so forth, at this age. We made sure we began looking at kids in elementary school so we could watch them move through this process of becoming more sex typed as they moved into adolescence. The data I described popped out at us. So we went back and checked, and, sure enough, in every district we were in, the kids went from sixth grade elementary school into seventh grade junior high school. This also means they experienced a building change and everything that goes with that building change. This then got us very interested in the question: Is it puberty or is it school change? Puberty and school change were co-occurring for these children between the sixth and seventh grades.

We went back to the literature to see if others were finding this same grade-level effect and if it was related to the transition. We started this work in the mid-1980s. We found that not very many people had looked at this question, so there was not a lot of evidence regarding the impact of the junior high school transition. Just as teachers specialize in secondary versus primary school, researchers specialize in childhood versus adolescence.

We had to piece together studies that looked at elementary school classrooms and studies that looked at junior high school classrooms. In the process, we had to compare very different methodologies— different measures of motivation, different measures of self-concept, and so forth. Studies usually reported that students were in the seventh grade—not what type of school they were in. So we didn't know if the kids were in a junior high school or a K-8 school (kindergarten through eighth grade). We tried to go back and get that information from the investigators when we could. Even so, forming an impression of how general the findings in our data were was very difficult.

From this jigsaw picture emerged the following results, the following profile, of kids making the transition to junior high. The list represents our guess at the developmental changes in motivation that might be associated with the transition into junior high school:

A decline in general interest in school

An increase in extrinsic motivational orientation for school work (meaning the children are now working for a grade or because their teacher told them to—not because they like it, or want to master it, or like challenging material)

A decrease in intrinsic motivational orientation for school work

A decline in general self-esteem

A decline in confidence in some academic disciplines—and here, math and science yield a fairly consistent pattern of decline

A decline in the subjective task value attached to some academic subjects (math and science in particular)

An increase in anxiety and in the relationship of anxiety to school performance and intrinsic motivation—not only are they reporting greater anxiety, but anxiety appears to be having a debilitating effect on their performance

A decrease in the relationship between academic performance and confidence in one's academic abilities

An increase in confusion regarding the causes of one's academic performance—so at the same time their anxiety is going up (and anxiety seems to be related to how well they are doing), their sense of how good they are as people seems to be becoming less related to how well they are doing in school

An increase in self-focused motivation—the children are focusing on what indicators of performance mean about their personal abilities—so, for example, rather than using grades to determine whether they need to learn more to do better next time, they are using grades to tell them whether or not they have ability

An increasing endorsement of the view that academic abilities are stable

Now, let me show you some examples of the studies that are showing this—and I've picked the best. The graphs in Figures 3.5a, 3.5b, and 3.5c are from some work by Susan Harter (1981). She used the same measure across grade level. She pits two motivational orientations against each other. She says some kids like challenge, whereas others prefer easy work, and asks kids which they are. You'll note that over the period of time from Grade 3 to Grade 9, they become more and more likely to check that they prefer easy work as opposed to challenging work. And again, you see this dip between sixth and seventh grades. I called her, and she said that, in her school districts, students made the transition from elementary to junior high school between grades six and seven. Note also the decline in curiosity versus teacher approval as well as the decline and the dip between sixth and seventh grades on the desire for independent mastery versus doing it to please the teacher.

Harter does her work in Denver, Colorado. Denver recently shifted its school system from a junior high school model to a middle-school model. There is currently, of course, a big movement toward middle schools. What that usually means is that schools change their grade structure and not much else. In other words, kids move to middle school at the end of the fifth grade instead of to junior high school at the end of the sixth grade. Because it's easy to do, this is often how schools purport to incorporate the middle school philosophy. It may look like they're doing something, but they often don't go on to do the necessary work to create a new environment. The middle school philosophy is really very different from the junior high philosophy. To make that shift meaningfully requires a tremendous amount of resocialization. One cannot take the same teachers and principals who ran the junior high school and have them run a middle school the next year without doing major in-service training to change the nature of the environment. Presumably, Denver was going to do this retraining.

A Denver newspaper, however, came out with some very interesting statistics. It looked at expulsion rates for sixth graders. It compared the rate when sixth grade was the last year in elementary school with the rate the next year when sixth grade became the first grade in middle school. Expulsion rates increased dramatically in that period of time. We know that expulsion rates are one of those indicators of entering the dropout track and certainly of falling behind in academic

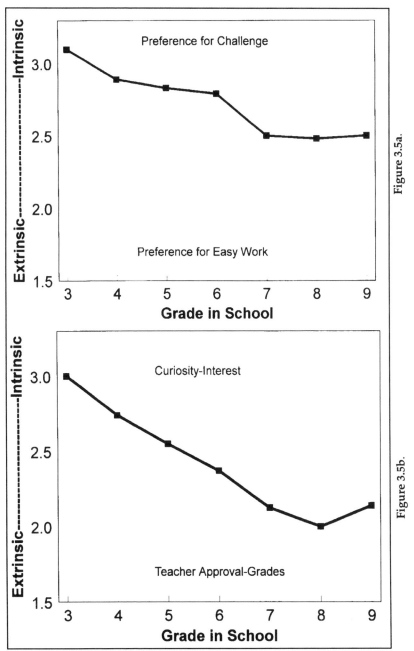

Figure 3.5a.

Figure 3.5b.

Figure 3.5. Grade Differences in Students' Motivational Orientation
SOURCE: Harter (1981), reprinted with permission.

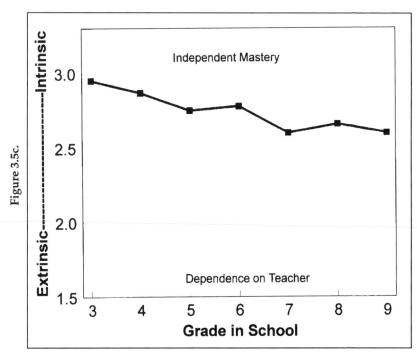

Figure 3.5. Continued

work. So, this wonderful shift that was to make the world better for these sixth graders resulted in more of them being kicked out of school for disciplinary reasons than had been the case under the old system!

Another study, work by Blyth and Simmons (Blyth & Simmons, 1978; Blyth, Simmons, & Carlton-Ford, 1983), looked specifically at those environments. They compared kids in a K-8 school with kids who were in a traditional junior high school. They looked at how involved kids were in extracurricular activity, for both males and females. In Figures 3.6a and 3.6b, you can see that moving to the seventh grade for the junior high cohort led to a decline in participation for both males and females. They became less involved with things that were going on in school.

In summary, Blyth and Simmons found the following negative effects of the structure of kindergarten through sixth grade (K-6) followed by Grades 7 through 9 versus the K-8 structure:

1. Girls' self-esteem declines

2. GPA declines

3. Extracurricular activities decline

4. Leadership roles decline

5. Boys' sense of being victimized increases

6. Feelings of anonymity increase

These findings are neither unique to our school system nor only true of the current situation. Simmons and her colleagues (Blyth, Simmons, & Bush, 1978; Blyth, et al., 1983) have done this study in three different school districts spread over approximately the last 15 years. Their first study was done at the beginning of the 1970s. Simmons and her colleagues found the six effects I just mentioned fairly consistently. Some other effects vary by school district.

And What Did We Find in Math Classrooms in Particular?

We have also studied changes in the school environment over the junior high school transition. In our work, we looked closely at what is going on in math classrooms in particular, and we followed the same children across time as they moved from sixth grade into seventh grade. The environmental changes that kids experienced with the junior high school transition that we observed in these math classrooms are these:

Increase in extrinsic motivational strategies

More rigorous grading practices resulting in lower average grades

Increase in practices likely to focus students' attention on ability assessment—ability grouping, whole class instruction, normative performance-based grading practices, and competitive motivational strategies

Increase in teachers' concern with control

Decrease in teachers' trust of students

Decrease in opportunity for student participation in classroom decision making

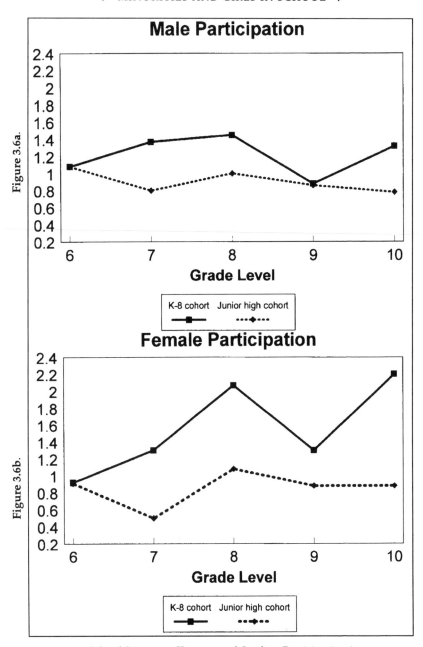

Figure 3.6. School Structure Changes and Student Participation in Extracurricular Activities
SOURCE: Blyth, Simmons & Bush (1978), reprinted with permission.

Decrease in student autonomy

Initial decrease in the cognitive level of the tasks required of students

Decrease in teachers' sense of efficacy

Imagine yourself making this type of transition. In the sixth grade, you had a teacher who trusted you, a teacher who gave you some autonomy and respect, and a teacher who felt confident about being able to motivate most everyone in the class. You were getting math material that was at a fairly complex level—proportions and so forth—and were getting a fairly good grade. You go to the seventh grade, and your grades drop, although the material is review. You thought you knew it last year, and now you're getting a lower grade than you got last year. Your grade seems to be based not on how much you learn over the course of the year but on your relative position to other kids in the class. Your teacher tries to motivate you primarily by stressing the need to do well on tests. You think you are growing toward adulthood and suddenly, you're trusted less and treated with less autonomy and respect. The material is essentially very repetitive in the way it is taught, and the classroom is very competitive. And you can't even choose where you sit! This is the modal experience that kids get in the seventh grade math classrooms.

In addition, your seventh grade teacher feels less efficacious than your sixth grade teacher. We asked the teachers in the sixth grade and the teachers in the seventh grade how confident they felt about being able to teach everyone in their class. What we found was—and this was the biggest difference we saw—that the seventh grade teachers were far less confident about their ability to reach everybody in their classes and far more certain that there were some groups of kids who would never learn math no matter what they did. This was true in spite of the fact that the seventh grade teachers were far more likely to be trained in math as their specialty.

Given this important difference, we wanted to assess its impact on the children's motivation. We broke the kids into two groups based on whether or not they did well in school when they were sixth graders, using their standardized test scores to make this judgment. We then looked at teacher efficacy. On the average, the teacher efficacy, as I said, drops from sixth grade to seventh grade. There were, however, some teachers at both levels with high and with low efficacy, so we could do a natural experiment. We could look at kids who moved from a teacher with a lot of confidence in his or her ability to a teacher without confidence. And we could look at all combinations of those two levels of teacher efficacy.

When we looked at the kids who were doing well in school, we found that the nature of the change of their teachers' efficacy had no effect on their self-perception. But for the kids in the bottom half of the class, this change made a lot of difference in their motivation, as you can see in Figures 3.7a and 3.7b.

In the first graph, the solid lines are kids who moved from a high-efficacy 6th-grade teacher to a low efficacy 7th-grade teacher, which is the transitional pattern for 50% of the kids. We measured the kids' estimates and expectancies for their own performance—two times in the 6th grade and two times in the 7th grade. The transition comes between the second and the third wave. Waves one and two are in the 6th grade; waves three and four are in the 7th grade.

As you can see, when the kids in the bottom half of the class experience the transition and go from a high-efficacy teacher to a low-efficacy teacher, their confidence in their own math ability drops. But when the kids in the bottom half of the class experience the transition and go from a high-efficacy teacher to a high-efficacy teacher, they essentially show a straight pattern—that is, they continue to be confident in their math abilities. Unfortunately, only about 20% of the kids experience that pattern.

If you look at Figure 3.7b, you can see some positive consequences. Moving to the 7th grade is not inevitably bad. If you go to a high-efficacy teacher in the 7th grade from a low-efficacy teacher in the 6th grade, your self-concept goes up. Notice, however, the consequences of going from a low-efficacy teacher to a low-efficacy teacher: Self-concept continues a downhill slide. These graphs, again, represent the low-achieving students. We found the change in teacher efficacy had no effect on the high-achieving students.

? What's Going on in Junior High Schools That is Causing This Problem?

The short answer is, we don't know. Some, including the writers of the recent Carnegie report (Task Force, 1989), have talked about the size of the institution as a cause of the problem: the fact that it is large

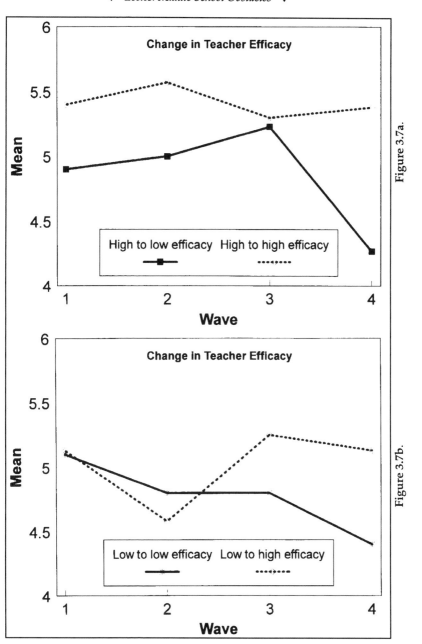

Figure 3.7a.

Figure 3.7b.

Figure 3.7. Changes in Low-Achieving Students' Expectations of their Performance as a Function of Changes in the Efficacy of Their Teachers. SOURCE: Adapted from Midgely, Feldlaufer, and Eccles (1989a).

and bureaucratic and teachers have to deal with so many kids at once so they don't get to know them. One of the big differences between the sixth grade in an elementary school and a seventh grade in a junior high school is that the 7th-grade teachers are confronted with having to teach 150 kids, which may be why they feel they have to control them so much. You can't get to know 150 kids, and if one kid is acting out, the only thing the teacher may feel he or she can do is to kick him or her out of the classroom. Teachers don't have the time or the personal commitment to know their students well enough to help them over their rough times.

To excel in math and science, in particular, students need that kind of contact. If kids don't understand math, they will quickly fall behind. If they don't feel they have a good relationship with their teachers, they won't feel like they can go for help. Consequently, they will soon find themselves hopelessly lost.

Another cause of the problem may be the stereotypes we have of adolescence. You know as well as I do the stereotypical view adults in our country have toward adolescents—they are out of control, they are "ornery." Some psychologists have even suggested that adolescents' rebellious behavior and obnoxious ways are inherited and reflect our primate ancestry! We asked teachers what they thought about adolescents, whether they thought adolescents were overwhelmed with hormones and incapable of learning at this particular period. Sure enough, many of the teachers believed this. And the longer they had been teaching in junior high school, the more likely they were to believe this about their kids. This may be less true of teachers who are in K-8 schools.

In the Carnegie report (Task Force, 1989), we tried to look at middle schools, taking some of these possible problem causes into account. What I want to emphasize is that even though the effect of the differences between grade school and middle school may have general effects across subject areas, the effects are more marked in math and science classes—that is, they have an even bigger effect on students' interest in those subjects. The Carnegie report suggests a whole series of alternative ways of thinking about middle school education. The recommendations are an attempt to answer this question: What kind of middle school education would you create for kids if you

Table 3.1 Design for an Optimal Middle School

1. Create a community for learning and development.
   Small groups (150-300)
   Teams of students and teachers who stay together throughout middle school years
      (5 teachers per 125 students)
   An adviser for each student who meets very regularly with each advisee

2. Teach a common core of knowledge to everyone.
   Assume all students can learn the material.
   Provide some opportunity for specialization as well.
   Use cooperative learning and peer tutoring.
   Take an interdisciplinary approach for core courses.

3. Ensure success for all students.
   Do not track by ability.
   Use alternative methods to adjust to ability-level differences.
   Cooperative learning
   Cross-age tutoring
   Flexible scheduling to provide varying amounts of time to master material
   Multiple learning opportunities to get additional help

4. Empower teachers and administrators.
   Give teachers greater flexibility in designing instruction.
   Create building-level governance committees.

5. Improve academic performance through better health.

6. Reengage families in schooling.
   Give parents a meaningful role.
   Help parents help their children.

7. Connect schools with communities
   Involve all youth in volunteer youth service.
   Connect schools with informal teaching programs out of school.
   Involve local businesses and community as resources for teachers and students.
   Expand career guidance programs and apprenticeships.

SOURCE: Adapted from Task Force (1989).

could design one optimally? I would urge you to consider carefully the seven points that are suggested in Table 3.1:

The first recommendation deals with the issue of size. We need to reduce the size of groupings, or at least the scale, to make sure kids have adequate contact with teachers in a consistent manner over several years of time. So, whatever we do for this age group, let's not put them into a factory. Let's put them into an environment where they can have close contact with a few teachers who get to know them well (the same way the elementary school teachers did), can monitor their progress, can work with them if they begin to fall behind, and can work with them if they show that they don't understand particular things. We can't tear down the junior high school buildings. What can we do instead? The Carnegie Task Force (1989) report suggests schools within schools. We're not going to be able to go back to elementary schools, but we can do schools within schools. We can create small communities within larger buildings and let that be the teaching-learning unit.

You'll note the recommendation not to track by ability. Consider this summary of findings on ability tracking:

Clear evidence of social class and ethnic group bias:

>Biased tests used for placement

>Biased screening and placement strategies

>Parents less likely to protest low group placement

Clear evidence that tracking undercuts achievement of students placed in low tracks

Tracking creates stratified social groups that, in turn, contribute to higher dropout rates and lower interest in math and science for students placed in low-ability tracks.

Teachers clearly treat students placed in different ability tracks differently; usually, these differences serve to widen the achievement gap between students in the high-ability and low-ability groups.

Track placement in math in junior high school affects curricular stream placement in high school.

Very little upward migration across tracks, even though one reason for ability differences at the point of assignment is different maturational rates—that is, birth date correlates with track placement.

Differences between Catholic school (CS) versus public school (PS):

>In CS, 72% of students in academic track versus only 38% of students in PS

>CS students greater than PS students in achievement, desire to go to college, and high school achievement

Association between social class and achievement is less for
CS students than PS students

The recommendation in the Carnegie (Task Force, 1989) report that
I think has the greatest potential in the short run for us in terms of
math and science is to connect schools with communities. We have to
get scientists into the schools, to work in the instructional system, not
as full-time teachers but to work with teachers on how to make science
and math exciting. I have sat in math and science classrooms, and I
can tell you they are deadly dull—even things as interesting as the
computer or science experiments can be turned into memory work.
It's no wonder the kids' interest wanes by the time they get to the
seventh grade. They have not been taught math in a user-friendly or
person-friendly format.

The one thing that is very clear from all the work we did with girls
in math and science is that the practices that work in math and science
classrooms are hands-on instruction and the opportunity to work on
real problems rather than made up problems. The students must come
to view math and science as tools, not theoretical systems. Use them
interdisciplinarily. Don't treat them as having nothing to do with
history and literature. An objective should be to integrate science and
math with other subjects so kids see the utility of science and math as
tools in domains other than simply science and math. Don't use
competitive instruction. Don't use drill and practice. Put kids into
teams. Let them work together, instruct each other, and do the experiments together—that works for girls, it works for minorities, it works
for everybody. But it's not often done.

I think an important way to achieve our goals in science and math
education is to break down the barrier between the school and the
community. The people who are best at thinking about science as a
tool are the people who aren't using it as a theoretical system, who
weren't trained in it as a theoretical system, but who were trained to
use it as a tool to solve real-world problems. People who know how
to use science and math this way need to come into the school systems
and help the teachers teach science and math that way.

Last, let me give you three other summaries to take with you, Tables
3.2, 3.3, and 3.4:

Table 3.2 Advantages of Small Schools, Particularly for At-Risk Students

Lower drop-out rates (2-3 times lower)

Less drug involvement (6 times less)

Less truancy (2 times less)

Lower suspension rates (2-3 times lower)

Less victimization at school

More involvement in school activities

Higher average achievement levels

Higher rates of positive academic engagement

Higher average levels of self-esteem

Higher average levels of perceived current opportunities and perceived future opportunities

Higher average sense of efficacy

Higher average sense of personal control

Higher rates of parent involvement

SOURCE: Adapted from Task Force (1989).

Table 3.3 Characteristics of Effective Classrooms

Frequent use of cooperative learning opportunities

Frequent use of individualized learning opportunities

Infrequent use of competitive motivational strategies

Frequent use of hands-on learning opportunities

Frequent use of practical problems as assignments

Active career and educational guidance aimed at broadening students' view of math and physical sciences

Frequent use of strategies designed to create full class participation

SOURCE: Adapted from Task Force (1989).

Table 3.4   Interventions to Increase Female and Minority
Participation in Mathematics and Science

Better teaching
  Female-friendly instruction
  Equitable access and experience

Better counseling
  Course enrollment advice
  Career advice regarding
    Types of occupations
    Need to be self-supporting

Better linkages with home
  Involve parents
  Inform parents of talents and relevant occupations

Provide better role models

Facilitate late reentry into nontraditional fields

Q; *I am interested in what you have to say about tracking as well as
gifted-and-talented programs.*

A; In addition to the summary of findings on ability tracking I
gave you, I can tell you that I have been looking at tracking in
our data. We have some kids who were tracked in the seventh
grade who are now seniors in high school, and we have seen
what happens to them as a consequence of having been tracked
in math in the seventh grade. It's a very interesting problem
because it has a different effect depending on whether you are
talking about students at the top or students at the bottom. The
general data on tracking—let's leave out the gifted and talented
for a moment—suggest the evidence is not very strong that the
kids at the top benefit from having been tracked. But the evidence is pretty clear that the kids at the bottom suffer from

91

having been tracked. There is very little movement across tracks even though we know, for example, that one of the best predictors of being tracked is birth date. So, if you happen to be the youngest kid in your class, you are much more likely to be tracked down than to be tracked up—for developmental reasons. But once you're tracked, it's very difficult for you to move out of the track. Tracking was originally designed to help get kids matched with the material they're capable of dealing with. But what we find is that in the lower tracks, the teachers lower the level of the material and the amount they teach. At the end of the year, those kids are farther behind than they were at the beginning of the year. When we looked at our kids, what we found was that the kids who were doing poorly in the 6th grade and ended up getting tracked in the 7th grade (compared to the kids who were doing poorly who were not tracked in the 7th grade) were more likely to have dropped out of school by the 10th grade, less likely to have any interest any longer in math and science, and more likely to be in a general or vocational track program. Essentially, they were steered out of the college track and were more likely to be involved in all kinds of deviant activities outside of school. So I say that is a cost, and it is one that is too great.

The kids at the top who were tracked did end up looking a bit better for having been tracked. They were slightly more likely to be in science. So is the cost at the bottom end worth the gain at the top end? I think that's the real issue in tracking. What I would suggest instead is contained in the Carnegie (Task Force, 1989) report: Let's do cross-ability, cross-age tutoring because we know that kids gain by teaching someone else. One of the best things you can do for gifted kids is to give them the opportunity to teach kids who need to be taught rather than tracking them and heading them down a different route from their peers. One learns a great deal by teaching. Most of the tutoring evidence suggests that the people who gain the most are the tutors. So we don't have to be concerned that our gifted kids are suffering as a consequence of tutoring other kids.

The other best data are contained in the summary I gave you earlier. Catholic schools on principle do not track, and they try to keep as high a proportion of their kids on the college track program as possible. They require that their students take college track courses and then require that they learn the material. Those schools have a much higher proportion of kids who end up on the college track when they get to high school, and those students have much lower dropout rates than non-Catholic-school students. And Catholic schools don't necessarily start with a higher caliber of kids. That is, their standardized test scores prior to entering such programs are not different from students who do not enter such programs.

Q: *I have believed for quite a while that we are primarily a product of expectations that others have of us.*

A: I agree that other people's expectations for us have a big impact. Those expectations come from everywhere—the media, our parents, our peers, our teachers. Comer (1990) specifically focused on the expectations of the schools. He said let's take an inner-city school—a hard-core school, one with a big dropout problem, a drug problem, and kids who are failing. He then tried to change the expectations of that school to see if kids' achievement could be affected. He very successfully did so. I have to emphasize that it does take a major shift in expectations by all authority figures. You really have to change the expectations of the school and of the parents. That really means you have to change the culture of that building. That's what I was talking about earlier. When you convert from a junior high school system to a middle school system, if all you do is shift the grade configuration, you shouldn't expect you are going to get any different outcome.

You can get kids turned around if you get the expectations changed. Indeed, you can get parents and teachers turned around as well. You can get them all on a track that says, what we're about here is learning math and science. *Everybody* can learn math and science. *Nobody* is not going to learn math and science in this building. Comer is successful at getting this type of change, although he has never focused particularly on math and science (Comer, 1990). But other schools have. There are good examples of principals around the country who have essentially taken this as their mandate and have turned things around through expectations.

What is interesting about the middle school is one of the things I hope I got across to you: We have these stereotypes about adolescents. Then we put them all in the building and—sure enough—they act just like we think they are going to act. They act out, they are disinterested, they stare off, they can't be trusted, they get in trouble when they go to the bathroom. I think expectations play a big role here. We set up an environment that is very alienating and not very personal at exactly the time when they most need adults, when they most need close contact with people who care about them and will watch them and will help them down a very difficult road. There are people outside the school trying to sell drugs, and it is a really tough developmental period. At this critical time, we withdraw all the supports. Because they function under a different set of expectations, the kids in the old K-8s don't act that way.

Q: *Your statistics reflect cultural diversity of the student body, but I don't notice any attention to cultural differences in the recommendations. I wonder what study there has been on that. My impression of many of the school systems these days is that teachers are really kind of reeling. Most of the teachers are from the mainstream, and their student bodies increasingly are recent immigrants, who are increasingly diverse. The teachers are having to deal with these differences in learning styles, languages, and so forth. I wonder to what extent that would affect your research.*

A: I don't want to minimize the problems of teachers in the United States today. I just came back from Europe where I looked at some schools in Holland. The fact that we are committed to getting everyone through the school system and through the same school system makes our problem much more difficult and much different than the problems being faced in other countries. I think some of the recommendations that are being suggested by the Carnegie (Task Force, 1989) report will make the job easier. By downscaling, creating cooperative teams, and moving power back to the teachers and parents, you potentially will be able to produce teams of people who are committed to these kids and are close enough to them to be able to tailor the instruction to their particular needs. That's one of the reasons the Carnegie report in particular didn't say to use this curriculum versus that curriculum. They specifically said that those decisions have to be made locally, taking into account the local needs. But what you have to do is get a team of people together to solve that problem who believe it can be solved.

The issue of getting more people interested in math and science is very different for women than it is for minorities. In the case of minorities, you're not just talking about developing an interest in math and science. You are also facing the more fundamental challenge to get them through the school system. And look at the problems: They attend schools where there is not a lot of money, schools that are beleaguered in other ways as well, schools where the teachers are overwhelmed. The problem in minority education is a much more difficult problem than getting girls interested in math and science. The girls, in many cases, are in the same schools as the White males who traditionally have entered math and science. So we begin with an advantage in solving their problem. We can make great headway just by changing the way math and science are taught in schools that have resources. But to tackle the problems presented by minority and immigrant education, we're going to have to do a lot more work. Not only does teaching have to be changed, but resources have to be allocated differently.

Q: *In many K-8 schools, the seventh and eighth grades are still treated as a different group within the institution. Based on your summary of the research, would you say it would be better to treat them just the same as the other classes?*

A: I think it is probably better to keep them together as a group so they aren't having different kids in every classroom. I think the critical issue is to let their social network stay together. Don't have them with so many different teachers that the teachers can't get to know them. Try to make it so they can have four

95

different teachers, but have those teachers, for example, stay with them for the sixth, seventh, and eighth grades. Or instead of having a seventh grade teacher and an eighth grade teacher, get a team of teachers: Have a math specialist, have a science specialist, have a reading specialist, but have them work with those kids for 3 years so they have a chance to know the kids well enough to keep close track of them. The issue is keeping close track of them, monitoring how they are doing both emotionally and academically, so they don't fall behind and feel so alienated that they can't go for help when they need it. That's what you have to do for kids of this age group.

Q: *You mentioned something about giving power back to the teachers. I wonder what you mean by that. I am one of those in a beleaguered school. I find that power is not being translated down into having teachers give more hours to instruction and less time to police duty. The community's interest doesn't seem to be in that direction. So I'm wondering what you mean by giving the power back to the teachers. It's hard to be a good teacher if you don't have the time to teach well. I wonder if perhaps the community just doesn't trust that teachers would use time to improve their teaching if they were given freedom from having to be cops.*

A: As one teacher to another, I'm sure that trust is lacking. The president of my university doesn't trust his faculty to use its time wisely! Again, the best example I can give you of giving power to the teachers is the Comer (1990) schools. What he means by it is literally to give the power back to the teachers. He creates teacher-parent-principal management teams. Not only is the team given the problems of the school, but they are also given the responsibility to deal with them—and the resources to take action. You don't have to increase the resources, but you have to give the management team access to the resources. The teams identify what the problems in the school are and what it will take to solve them. Clearly, this approach will initially take more time than teachers normally now spend. But once it is in place, it should be a lot more fun and rewarding than when someone else was calling the shots. You really have to be willing to let go and let it happen. It's going to fail in some cases. But what more and more people are suggesting is that it is worth the risk because what we're doing right now is not working very well either.

There are a lot of barriers, and the Carnegie report (Task Force, 1989) does deal with some of these things. A whole set of these barriers has to do with trust—who trusts or does not trust whom. I think we have to break down barriers between teachers and parents because I think teachers don't want parents meddling in the schools just as parents don't want teachers meddling in the home. The first thing that always comes up is that one group wants to blame the other: The teachers blame the parents or the administrators, the parents blame the teachers or the administrators, the administrators blame the teachers and parents. At some point, you have to have these groups come together. They all have a vested interest—the kids. We can't worry about who is responsible for what. We have to solve the problem now, together. The other thing that the Carnegie report really talks about is breaking down the barrier between the school and the informal learning community. Learning doesn't start at the school gate. What you really have to do is get the community involved, which may eventually help solve the problem of the people who say, "I don't have anything to do with school so why should I put my money there." If they themselves are invested in what is going on at the school building, maybe they will be more sympathetic when it comes to voting. But it also means you can take advantage of some other resources. One tactic, for example, that the Carnegie report suggests is to have every child in the middle school involved in some kind of community service. Learning occurs on the job as well as at school. Schools need to work to get that coordinated.

Q: *Have you looked at the number of women who go into math and science who come out of single-sex schools? Is there a difference?*

A: Yes, there is a difference for women in the United States as shown in the data. But I should note that the sociology of single-sex schools is unusual in this country compared to other countries. So we have real problems trying to understand what the selection process was that got kids into the single-sex schools in the first place in the United States. In fact, the best studies on single-sex schools are done in Australia and to some extent England, where such schools are more clearly an option. Because they are a more routine option there, they don't produce a very biased, skewed sample as is the case here. And what those studies suggest is that girls are more likely to go on in atypical fields if they are in single-sex schools than if they are in coed schools. Males from single-sex schools, however, are more likely to come out sex typed and to hold more sexist attitudes than they would had they gone to a coed school. So the best option is to let girls go to single-sex schools but make all boys go to coed schools, if we go strictly by the data! I don't think we should go strictly by the data. The point I want to make is that we know enough now about how to teach math and science that we don't need to have single-sex schools. What seems to happen in single-sex schools is that those girls are more likely to get mentored and less likely to be hassled by their male peers about what they're doing. You can create an environment in a coed school that produces that effect for both the males and the females if you work at it. We can take what we learned from single-sex schools to design better programs in coed schools. For example, we can make sure there is an adequate number of females in classes—that is, no one is scheduled for isolation. We can make it clear to the teacher that equal amounts of time are to be spent with the boys and the girls, and that doesn't mean spending the time with the girls patting them on the back and spending the time with the boys giving them experiences with the equipment. We can make sure girls get leadership roles.

Q: *How do we compare internationally other than by achievement exam— for example, attitudes toward math and science?*

A: There is that same old problem of different studies using different measures, which makes it difficult to make comparisons across nations. We do know that the amount of sex difference in performance varies across countries, and we're not exactly sure why. We only have the data; we haven't looked at the classrooms to see what is going on. We know that some cultures have a higher proportion of both males and females who go on in math and sciences than in the United States, and there clearly are differences in the expectations. For example, in many countries, it is expected that everyone will take physics; it's not an option, whereas in our schools it is. In some countries, one is expected to take 4 years of math, whereas here one is expected to take only 2 years to graduate.

Q: *Are you saying that if we make the change at the end of the 8th grade instead of at the end of the sixth, we'll minimize the change and not just delay it? And have you looked at all at the change from junior high school to high school?*

A: The data (Blyth, Simmons, and Bush 1978; Blyth, et al., 1983) clearly suggest that some of the negative consequences of the transition to junior high school are repeated at the transition to high school. What you have to realize is that kids who go to middle school or junior high school essentially have two transitions. They have to make a second transition when they go into high school. The Blyth, Simmons and Bush data suggest that K-8 kids maintain their advantage through the high school years. There is a transition effect, but they continue to maintain their advantage. It also appears that some of the kids who made the junior high school transition react even worse to the high school transition.

I would like to argue that it is not the transition that is most damaging. I don't think that whether kids stay in the same building or go to a different building is really what matters. What matters is what happens in those buildings. K-8s look better because seventh and eighth grades in K-8s are a better environment than seventh and eighth grades in junior highs. But you can produce a seventh and eighth grade experience in a junior high school building that has the positive aspects of the seventh and eighth grade experience in the K-8s. So again, what is important is the environment they move from and the environment they move to; it's not the transition. I don't think it matters whether they make it in sixth grade, whether they make it in fifth grade, or whether they make it at eighth grade. All these arguments about how much it is in sync with puberty I think are probably missing the point.

Q: *Would you argue that high school students would also do better in a smaller environment?*

A: Yes. Don't we? And it's true for the transition into college. You would be surprised at how many people I talk to who have a child in a high school with 3,000 kids who tell me they want their child to go to a small liberal arts college so they can have close contact with their teachers. That's a transition at age 18 or 19 years, and they want to put their kids in a college that is smaller than the high school they had no objection to. Downsized environments, we know from organizational psychology, are much easier to deal with. What is interesting is that we have known this for a long time. For example, we know that in organizations where someone has to manage many, many people that what seems to happen fairly regularly is that the manager begins to lose trust in the people he or she manages and assumes the workers are likely to try to get away with things and to try to make the manager look bad—exactly the things the 7th and 8th-grade teachers tell us about their kids. We shouldn't be surprised that we see these effects in adolescents because we know they are true for adults. Why would we expect anything more mature to happen?

Q: *My daughter went from a K-8 program into high school. The K-8 was good, but being a 9th grader in the same building with seniors (who are 18 or 19 years old) was enormously overwhelming for her. I think she would have been better off if she had one more year before the transition.*

A: I think it's amazing how many people think however they have it now is exactly the way it should be. My daughter switched from a junior high to a middle school, and she told me how awful it was going to be to have 6th-grade kids in her school! I really don't think the timing is all that critical. What is critical is what happens on both sides of that shift. We need to make an environment that is on a human scale, that gives teachers and students an opportunity to know each other well enough that they can trust each other, especially given our stereotypes.

I go out and talk to people in school districts on a fairly regular basis. A lot of districts are trying to make a decision now whether to move to the middle school concept and so forth. It is a big issue, even more so now that the Carnegie report (Task Force, 1989) has come out. I am a sociologically oriented psychologist, so I think the structure of the environment has a tremendous impact. I think if I had to gamble on an environment that is likely to work, it would be the K-8. It has an environment that can't be produced in a middle school or a junior high school. The K-8 has the right structure. It's a smaller group of people. You don't have the same chances of it going wrong. You don't have so many things you have to watch for. But I tell people that and, amazingly enough, parents say to me I don't want 7th and 8th graders in the same building as my fourth grader. I remind them that their 4th grader is going to be a 7th and 8th grader someday and ask them if they don't want their child at that time to be in the best possible environment. But they still have this tremendous sense of protectiveness—to protect against the corruptive nature of those older children. Again, there is the stereotype that adolescents are somehow going to undermine and lead these kids down a bad path. The data don't suggest that is true. In fact, kids in 7th and 8th grades become a wonderful resource. They can do cross-age tutoring. They can have this really active role and feel they are cooperating with the teachers and administration, so they don't have to do graffiti on the walls. They really can become a resource and an asset to the building.

Q: *Why should the transition to middle school be more debilitating in math than in English or history?*

A: I think it's because the transition in the way math and science are taught is more dramatic than for English or history. My perception is that the way math is taught in the seventh grade—

and this may be true for the sciences as well—undercuts a lot of kids' motivation. It tends to be highly competitive, highly drill-and-practice oriented, and less cooperative. In fact, if you looked at what the kids got to do in their math classroom in the sixth grade compared to what they got to do in their math classroom in the seventh grade, you would find it much more boring and regimented and the teacher much more controlling in Grade 7. I think this is much less true in other subjects. For example, in English, the kids go from spelling lists and reading essentially to each other to really looking at literature and starting to have discussions and higher-level interactions with material.

Q: *You don't think it is anything about the material itself?*

A: Not at the 7th Grade. I would believe that if in the 7th Grade they started to get theoretical math, but they don't. The 7th Grade math curriculum is essentially a review of K-6, so there is not an abrupt change in its complexity. In fact, it's becoming more repetitive. By 8th Grade, some of that starts to change. Some kids get to go into prealgebra, depending on school district. But for others, 8th Grade becomes a review of K-7—more review, and yet their grades drop each year. So I think it's that combination of things I talked about earlier: There is much more full class instruction, it is much more obvious who is doing poorly and who is doing better, and the teachers are really pushing on the kids that they have to prepare for tests (for extrinsic reasons). Laurie Brush (1978, 1980) did a comparison of math and English classrooms and found this form of instruction much more characteristic of math classrooms than of English. It is not surprising that she also found that kids turned off more to math than they did to English.

Q: *Why do kids in so many other countries do better than kids in the United States?*

A: One of the reasons is many countries track out kids, so those who take the tests are a more select group. They are not a broad sample of the entire population. Often, at 11 years of age, kids who are going on to the college track are in one school, whereas kids who are going on to the vocational track are in a different school and may not be taking the test. But the second issue is that they spend a whole lot more time getting instruction in math. There is no question (and this is based again on a variety of time-use studies in classrooms in European and Oriental cultures) that all the way through elementary school, the kids are taught more math than our kids are.

Q: *Perhaps you hit the nail on the head when you said some U.S. schools only require 2 years of math to graduate from high school. Maybe the solution is to require more math and science.*

A: There certainly have been people who have suggested that. If you want to equate the amount of math training that females, minorities, and males get, require the same of everybody. And the Catholic schools do that. Some of the data comparing private and public schools suggest that one of the major differences is that there is less choice in the private schools. More people are expected to complete the college-bound curriculum than is true in standard public schools.

•◆••◆••◆•

References

Blyth, D. A., Simmons, R. G., & Bush, D. (1978). The transition into early adolescence: A longitudinal comparison of youth in two educational contexts. *Sociology of Education, 51*(3), 149-162.

Blyth, D. A., Simmons, R. G., & Carlton-Ford, S. (1983). The adjustment of early adolescents to school transitions. *Journal of Early Adolescence, 3*(1-2), 105-120.

Brush, L. R. (1978). A validation study of the mathematics anxiety rating scale (MARS). *Educational and Psychological Measurement, 38*(2), 485-490.

Brush, L. R. (1980). The significance of students' stereotype of a mathematician for their career planning. *Personnel and Guidance Journal, 59*(4), 231-235.

Chipman, S. F., & Thomas, V. G. (1984). *The participation of women and minorities in mathematical, scientific and technical fields.* Unpublished manuscript commissioned by the Committee on Research in Mathematics, Science, Technology and Education of the National Research Council, Washington, DC.

Comer, J. (1990). Home, school and learning. In J. Goodlad & P. Keating (Eds.), *Access to knowledge: An agenda for our nation's schools* (pp. 23-42). New York: College Entrance Examination Board.

Harter, S. (1981). A new self-report scale of intrinsic versus extrinsic orientation in the classroom: Motivational and informational components. *Developmental Psychology, 17*(3), 300-312.

Midgely, C., Feldlaufer, H., & Eccles, J. (1989a). Change in teacher efficacy and student self- and task-related beliefs in mathematics during the transition to junior high school. *Journal of Educational Philosophy, 81*(2), 247-258.

Midgely, C., Feldlaufer, H., & Eccles, J. (1989b). Student/teacher relations and attitudes toward mathematics before and after the transition to junior high school. *Child Development, 60*(4), 981-992.

Rutherford, F. J., & Ahlgren, A. (1990). *Science for all Americans*. New York: Oxford University Press.

Task Force on Education of Young Adolescents. (1989). *Turning points: Preparing American youth for the 21st century*. Washington, DC: Carnegie Council on Adolescent Development.

Task Force on Women, Minorities, and the Handicapped in Science and Technology. (1988, September). *Changing America: The new face of science and engineering, interim report*. Washington, DC: Author.

Vetter, B. M. (1981). Women scientists and engineers: Trends in participation. *Science,* 214, 4527, 18 December, 1313-1321.

Vetter, B. M. (1989, December). *Professional women and minorities: A manpower data resource service*. Washington, DC: Commission on Professionals in Science and Technology.

· 4 ·

What Stops Women and Minorities From Choosing and Completing Majors in Science and Engineering?

Nancy Betz

ABOUT THIS CHAPTER

In the preceding chapters, we have looked at desegregation, the major tool the country has used to bring equity to educational opportunity; at home influences that offer some promise of saving minority children from the worst effects of adverse experiences in school; and at the middle school, the bottleneck in schooling for many girls and members of minority groups. This examination of aspects of the schooling of girls and minority students has a "So what?" attached to it. That is, there are lifelong consequences of failing or succeeding to enable these individuals. Nancy Betz finishes our series by looking at the "So what?" It is a fact that women and members of minority groups enter fields of science and engineering with far less frequency than do their White male counterparts. The frequency with which these underrepresented groups enter these highly skilled professions is a good marker of their general enablement. When women and minority group members begin to enter these fields in numbers that represent their proportion in the general population, then we can begin to feel comfortable that efforts to enable them have succeeded. We aren't there yet.

Of course, the impediments presented in the elementary and secondary years—the shortcomings of poorly implemented desegregation, the home environments that do not prepare children to withstand harsh educational environments, and the educational environments themselves that sometimes do more to limit than to guarantee opportunity—are sufficient to make college attendance only a remote possibility for many. But college itself presents obstacles that are considerable and that are not limited to the challenge presented by the academic material. Thus, only the tiniest fraction of girls and minority students who enter the educational pipeline in kindergarten remain in that pipeline at the end of graduate school. What happens to these students in colleges and universities, and what could be done to make their college years most productive? That is the story told by Nancy Betz's research.

———————— •◆• ————————

*T*he underrepresentation of women and minority group members in science and engineering has been a chronic problem in this country, but in recent years, there has been considerable interest in how to deal with it. In this discussion, I will briefly outline the scope of the problem of underrepresentation of women and non-Asian minorities in careers in the sciences and engineering. Following that, I will discuss the barriers to women and minority students both in their initial choice of, and then their retention in, science and engineering majors in colleges and universities. I will conclude with recommendations for further research and for educational interventions and federal policy. But let me first acknowledge the work of agencies such as the National Academy of Sciences, the Office of Technology Assessment (which, sadly, Congress recently abolished), and the National Research Council in gathering and reporting basic data about these issues.

I would like to begin by mentioning that I have always had a particular interest in this topic because I was one of the girls lost to the "harder" sciences by virtue of sexist counseling and advising. I had been strongly interested in math and science as a kid and took a full load of high school science and math, through physics and calculus. I was, not surprisingly, the only girl in my 12th grade advanced math class and one of the few girls in my high school who remained in science through physics. I tentatively planned to major in chemistry, with a career in either research or medicine. I was accepted by MIT and several strong liberal arts colleges. Unfortunately, my high school guidance counselor advised me against medical school or graduate school because, as he said, they would be hard to combine with marriage and a family. And a teacher I respected advised me against MIT, suggesting that liberal arts backgrounds were much more useful for girls and that liberal arts would not be adequately developed at a school like MIT. So I went to a liberal arts school, still intending a chemistry and premed major. After some further sexist treatment by the faculty member who had been assigned as my adviser, I gave up and changed my major to psychology so I could fulfill my biological destiny to help people! I did not become the physical scientist I originally had in mind, but I have done a lot of thinking about, and research on, why I and others like me didn't. So I really didn't become the helper my adviser had in mind, either, but rather, a psychologist very interested in the underrepresentation of women and minority group members in the sciences. Incidentally, I am going to use the term *sciences* as a generic term, instead of *science and engineering*, which is a mouthful.

A Look at the Numbers

Women and non-Asian minorities are underrepresented in science occupations in comparison to their representation in the labor force, based on the most recent report from the National Science Board (1996). Although women constitute 45% of workers, they are only 30%

Table 4.1   Proportion of Women and Minority Doctoral Recipients in Various Science and Engineering Fields (1988, U.S. Citizens, by percentage)

Field	Women	Asian	Black	Hispanic
Physical sciences	17	3	1	2
Mathematics	16	5	<1	1
Computer science	11	7	<1	<1
Life sciences	33	3	2	2
Psychology	55	1	4	3
Social sciences (excluding psychology)	33	3	4	3
Engineering	7	8	1	2
Science and engineering doctorates	25	6	2	2

SOURCE: Adapted from NSF (1990).

NOTE: Native Americans earn fewer than .4% of baccalaureates and .2% of doctorates, so their numbers are as yet too small to warrant disaggregation by field.

of scientists and 4% of engineers. Blacks are 10% of workers but only 2% of scientists and engineers. Hispanics are 7% of the labor force and 1.8% of scientists and engineers. Native Americans are less than 1% of the labor force and about one fifth of 1% of scientists and engineers. Asian Americans are relatively well represented, constituting 2% of the labor force but 5% of scientists and engineers.

The pipeline for entrance to careers in science and engineering is obviously the colleges and universities, including graduate as well as undergraduate education. So it is the relative lack of participation there that is of particular interest to me. Table 4.1 shows the representation of women and minority members among doctoral degree recipients in 1988. As can be seen, the problem is particularly serious in the physical sciences and engineering, less so in the biological and quantitative sciences, and not at all in the social sciences and psychology.

A related problem is the general decline in the number of students selecting science majors. At the same time, we estimate a 27% increase in the number of science-based jobs and a 36% increase in the number of jobs requiring significant math background by the year 2000. The September-October 1989 issue of the *American Scientist* raised serious concerns about our undergraduates' declining interest in science (Green, 1989). Between 1966 and 1988, the proportion of college freshmen planning to major in the sciences and math fell by half, from 11.5% to 5.8%. Also, the sciences have the highest defection rates of any undergraduate major and the lowest rates of recruitment from other fields. Furthermore, demographic trends predict for the 1990s a significant drop in the number of White males of college age, who have been the dominant participants in the sciences. The likely effects of this drop and the declining interest are that the pool of science and engineering bachelor's degrees will decline by 26% by the late 1990s. It is this pool of baccalaureate degree holders from which our graduate students come, our future master's and doctoral-level scientists and engineers. Thus, we simply cannot afford to waste two large potential supplies of scientific talent and energy, those represented by women and minority group members.

Choice and Implementation in the Careers of Women and Minority Group Members

Why are women and minority people underrepresented in science careers? I am a vocational psychologist, so I talk in terms of two major phases of career development: choice and implementation. *Choice* is what you choose; *implementation* is how you get the educational training to implement your choice. Research findings can be organized in terms of these two major initial phases of the career development process. In terms of career choices, too few women and minority people are choosing the sciences in the first place. But the problem is especially serious among young women. In terms of the implementation of a career choice, which in the present case is done via undergraduate and, ideally, graduate degrees, retention is a serious problem. For women, problems in retention arise especially at the graduate degree level, where their degree attainment rate is lower than that of comparably able men. For minority students, academic and financial problems as well as problems related to the institutional environment seriously affect retention at both baccalaureate and graduate levels. In other words, we lose a lot of people in the educational pipeline.

The Role of Mathematics in Choice

There are two major barriers to a given choice: lack of preparation and lack of motivation or interest. As far as preparation is concerned, majoring in the sciences requires that one have a strong high school record, especially in math and science courses. In fact, college science majors are academically stronger students in high school than are majors in other fields. Failure to obtain adequate precollege preparation has been one of the major barriers for both women and minority students. Although women get better grades than men in both high school and college, they more often lack the math prerequisites for getting started in a science major in college. Math has been called the *critical filter* in career development; it filters out options in dramatic fashion.

The classic study of math as the critical filter to career options was done by Lucy Sells (1982). In a study of freshmen at the University of California at Berkeley, Sells found that only 8% of the women, versus 57% of the men, had taken 4 years of high school math. Four years of high school math were a prerequisite to entering the calculus or intermediate statistics courses required in three fourths of the possible scientific major field areas, and the university did not provide remedial courses to allow a student to complete the prerequisites after arriving there. Thus, 92% of the freshmen women at Berkeley were prevented by lack of math background from even considering 15 of the 20 major fields offered in science! The 5 remaining options were predictable—such traditionally female majors as the social sciences. Thus, decisions to "choose" these majors may in many cases have been by default, through failure to qualify for any major requiring math background.

Although women have been taking more math in recent years, they are still significantly less likely than young men to have completed the 4th year of high school math, usually a calculus or precalculus course. They are also significantly less likely to have taken high school physics, even though their participation in biology and chemistry courses has increased. Participation in physics may be particularly important because this is where interests in engineering careers are often born. High school women often report being tracked away from both physics and computer science courses. Even males who fall into the lower half of the achievement distribution are more likely than are females to continue the study of math and science.

There are many postulated reasons for the failure of females to continue taking math in high school and college. Most relate in some

Table 4.2 Percentages of Mathematically Gifted Boys and Girls Later Achieving Various Educational Levels (From Project Talent Follow-Up)

Highest Degree	Male		Female	
	Number	Percentage	Number	Percentage
PhD	64	32	10	6
MS	59	29	40	23
BA or BS	60	30	87	50
High school diploma	17	9	37	21
Total	200		174	

SOURCE: Adapted from Lubinski & Humphreys (1990).

way to perceptions that math is a male domain, that females aren't good at math, that females don't need math. Also lacking are role models and encouragement toward math achievement and careers. Suffice it to say that continuing efforts to encourage (or force) girls, especially high-ability girls, to continue in math is *essential* to keep open their option to pursue science careers.

To give you some idea of how much female mathematical talent we're losing, look at Table 4.2. It shows the highest degrees later obtained by mathematically gifted boys and girls. These were kids whose math achievement scores were at or above the 99th percentile in the Project Talent sample, a longitudinal study of about 100,000 kids in each of the high school grades (Benbow, 1988). Note that whereas 32% of mathematically gifted boys obtained doctorates, only 6% of mathematically gifted girls did. In contrast, 9% of the boys, but 21% of the girls, stopped with high school. This is clearly a tragic waste of talent.

Another example can be found in a study of mathematically precocious youth done at Johns Hopkins University. Of those who went on to graduate school, 42% of the boys and 22% of the girls went into the sciences (Lubinski & Humphreys, 1990). Again, these are gifted young people. The boys are pursuing science at a much greater level and are getting much higher degrees than are the girls. It is a loss we really need to stem, for the benefit of individuals as well as our society.

Although inadequate math and science course work limits women's choices, inadequate high school preparation in general limits the choices of minority students even more seriously, making surviving college-level course work difficult. Comparatively speaking, it's not the initial choices of minority students that keep them out of science but their retention in undergraduate and graduate degree programs. I'll come back to this later.

Psychological Barriers to Choice

Psychological barriers to the pursuit of scientific and technical careers also account for large losses of women and minority people to these fields. These barriers to women's and minority group members' choice of science careers can be viewed as maladaptive cognitions or beliefs about themselves in relationship to science, math, and technological careers. I have been interested in three general classes of such maladaptive cognitions: (a) gender or racial stereotypes or stereotypes of scientists, (b) low science-related self-efficacy expectations, and (c) beliefs that they wouldn't enjoy science. Research concerning these maladaptive cognitions suggests serious negative effects on women's choices of science careers.

Math, science, and technical fields have always been perceived as male-dominated fields. Psychological research has shown us that children as young as 2½ know which jobs are for women and that stereotyping increases with the age of the child. Furthermore, stereotypes are consistent with children's early choices for themselves. In several studies, the large majority of girls give nurse or teacher as their occupational choice, whereas boys give a much wider range of traditionally male occupations representing the sciences, trades, and professions. Girls limit themselves right off the bat in terms of what they will consider. Some girls and young women may avoid careers they perceive as male-dominated because they fear disapproval from others.

Stereotypical Roles

One study illustrating the power of occupational stereotypes was that of Drabman et al. (1981). The study used a videotaped portrayal of a 7-year-old boy going to visit his doctor. The doctor was a woman (named "Mary Nancy" to double the sex-salience of the name), and she was assisted by a male nurse named "David Gregory." Immediately after viewing the tape, children were given a multiple-choice quiz on which they were asked to recognize the names of the doctor and the nurse. In addition to the correct name, the distracters included a wrong same-sex name, the name of the opposite-sex character in the videotape, and a "wrong" opposite-sex name. In naming the doctor and the nurse, almost all 1st grade and 4th grade children assigned a gender-typed name, even if it was a name that hadn't appeared in the videotape at all. Only 4% of both 1st graders and 4th graders chose a female name for the doctors—41% of 1st graders chose the wrong male name rather than the correct female name. The authors conclude, distressingly, that children alter their perception or memory of a counterstereotyped videotaped presentation to fit their stereotypes.

Science itself elicits a particular kind of stereotype from people of all ages. Studies show that about 90% perceive scientists as old and White, usually with glasses and at least half of the time bearded. Here is a summary by Mead and Metraux (1957) of the views of scientists of about 35,000 high school students:

> The scientist is a brain. He spends his days indoors, sitting in a laboratory, pouring things from one test tube into another. His work is uninteresting, dull, monotonous, tedious, time consuming. . . . He may live in a cold water flat. . . . His work may be dangerous. Chemicals may explode. He may be hurt by radiation or may die. If he does medical research, he may bring home disease, or may use himself as a guinea pig, or may even accidentally kill someone. . . . He is so involved with his work that he doesn't know what is going on in the world. He has no other interests and neglects his body for his mind. . . . He has no social life, no other intellectual interests, no hobbies or relaxations. He bores his wife. . . . He brings home work and also bugs and creepy things. (p. 387)

Children of the 1980s hold images of science and scientists that are essentially unchanged from those of the 1950s. In 1986, researchers at Harvard University's Educational Technology Center applied Mead and Metraux's methodology to another generation of potential scientists. They reported the following:

> Most responses sounded familiar: Scientists are nerds and science is important but boring. The students had little inkling of the day-to-day intellectual activities of scientists, of what experiments are for, or of the social nature of the scientific enterprise.
> Stereotypes of this kind can have several types of detrimental effects. (Harvard Education Letter, 1988, p. 6)

Anyone who believes this will want to avoid science. Minority students may avoid career areas that they perceive as essentially closed to them, affirmative action notwithstanding. Both women and minority students may avoid career areas where they perceive they'll be one of the few or only members of their gender or race (or both). And because occupational stereotypes reflect the realities of gender and racial segregation in the occupational world, there *are* many fewer female and minority role models for girls and minority members to emulate. And just in case the young person's own stereotypes don't deter him or her, we can always throw in a sexist or racist high school guidance counselor to help matters. Although there are many excellent high school guidance counselors, research has shown us that many of them hold typical gender and racial stereotypes.

The Role of Guidance Counselors

Research has shown that the advice given by guidance counselors to clients often tends to encourage young women to stay in traditional roles (e.g., those of wife and mother) or to pursue traditionally female-dominated careers rather than a broader range of career options. In one early study by Pietrofessa and Schlossberg (1970), counselor trainees were asked to advise a female "client" (actually a research subject) wanting advice in choosing between her two top career preferences, engineering and education. Of preferential statements made by the counselors, over 80% were in favor of education and against engineering. Counselors said things such as "Engineering is normally thought of as a man's field," "If you were a teacher you could have your afternoons and summers off to be with your kids," and

"Engineering is awfully technical and doesn't give you a chance to help people." Can you imagine a counselor saying any of this to a young male student?

There are also a number of studies documenting the tendency of counselors to suggest a "downscaling of aspirations" to both young women and minority students—that is, suggest that options they are considering (e.g., the sciences) are pretty tough and demanding and may make it hard to have a personal life. Rather than a downscaling of aspirations, women and minority students considering science and engineering careers are probably in need of what has been called *decision support*. The more nonstereotypical the choice, the riskier it is for most women or minority members because they are venturing into White male territory. Thus, they need relatively more reassurance and support.

A Self-Efficacy Approach to the Aspirations of Girls and Minority Students

My own research has concerned the area of maladaptive cognitions called *low expectations of self-efficacy*, in particular, low self-efficacy with respect to science, engineering, and math-related fields. Along with my colleagues, I have been applying a theory introduced by Albert Bandura of Stanford University in 1977 for the study of gender differences in educational and career decisions (Bandura, 1977).

Figure 4.1 illustrates Bandura's model of perceived self-efficacy. Self-efficacy is our beliefs about our competence to engage in a certain domain of behavior. It is theorized by Bandura that self-efficacy determines whether we engage in a behavior in the first place, how well we perform, and whether we persist when we come to obstacles. He proposes that self-efficacy expectations, or our beliefs about our own competence with respect to specific domains of behavior, are the major mediators of approach versus avoidance (or choice) behavior and of the persistence of behavior when obstacles are confronted. Thus, self-efficacy is postulated to influence both initial choices and the persistence of behavior. We all have beliefs about our competence in different areas of behavior, and most of us will avoid areas where we feel incompetent, even if in reality we could perform the behavior

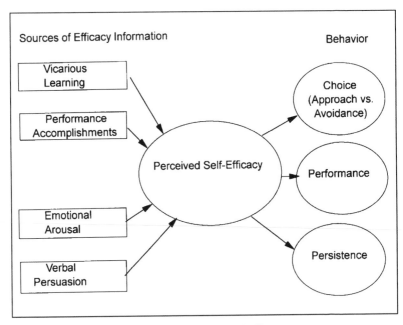

Figure 4.1. Bandura's Model of Perceived Self-Efficacy
SOURCE: Adapted from Bandura (1977).

if we tried. Some of us avoid math, public speaking, or other social interactions at least in part because we doubt our competence. I long avoided household repair jobs because, having been socialized to believe that women were all thumbs, I believed myself incompetent to change a fuse or a tire.

In theory, self-efficacy expectations are initially developed and subsequently modified by four sources of what Bandura called efficacy information—(a) performance accomplishments (experiences of successfully performing the given behavior), (b) vicarious learning or modeling (observing others successfully performing the behavior, especially others like us in some important ways), (c) freedom from anxiety with respect to the behavior, and (d) verbal persuasion and support from others. For example, successfully doing math, seeing that similar others (e.g., same sex) are good at math, control of feelings of anxiety toward math, and being encouraged to attempt math course work would lead to strong math-related efficacy, which would, in turn, lead to increased involvement and persistence in math.

People also need sufficient underlying ability and the motivation to engage in behavior. The self-efficacy theory does not say ability is irrelevant. The theory, however, is especially useful in understanding the underuse of real abilities on the part of such groups as women and minorities. Gail Hackett and I formulated a self-efficacy model to explain women's underrepresentation in male-dominated career areas (Hackett & Betz, 1981). We suggested that women's socialization led to insufficient exposure to sources of information that would lead to the development of strong expectations of efficacy with respect to many traditionally male-dominated career fields, particularly those in the sciences and technology. Similarly, the backgrounds of minority people may also be lacking in efficacy information. Blacks, for example, may lack role models of Black college grads, not to mention Black scientists and engineers; they may not have been encouraged to pursue science and math and may therefore lack a strong history of performance accomplishments. Again, self-efficacy theory may be helpful in explaining the avoidance of science and engineering careers.

Low self-efficacy expectations also lead to vicious cycles of avoidance. Let's say we have a young woman whose low expectations of self-efficacy lead her to avoid math course work. Obviously, avoidance of math courses is detrimental to her ability to perform math. So, when she is forced to confront it, she naturally performs poorly. If, for example, she then starts grad school in psychology and has to take statistics, her performance suffers, validating her beliefs that she is incompetent in math. At the first sign of failure, she wants to give up because she has no enduring belief that she can actually succeed. In contrast, a person with higher efficacy expectations regarding math would take math, not avoid it, be better prepared for math courses and tests, not be so anxious in those situations, and would persist longer if failure was encountered. The relationship of belief in oneself to persistence of behavior is well illustrated by the children's story of *The Little Engine That Could,* whose theme as it chugged up the hill was, "I think I can, I think I can."

In a series of studies, Hackett and I reported data suggesting that college-age women had significantly lower efficacy expectations with respect to math-based and science-based career fields, in comparison to equally able men (Betz & Hackett, 1981). For example, in one sample of 250 college students with equivalent American College Testing

117

(ACT) scores, 70% of the men but only 30% of the women reported that they believed they had the ability to complete a degree in engineering. Now, the fact is that neither 70% nor 30% is probably an accurate estimate of the number of students who could complete an engineering degree—some of the men may have been overestimating their abilities, whereas many of the women are underestimating theirs. But if an error is to be made, overestimating oneself means that one might try and fail, but underestimators may never try at all.

We also found that expectations of self-efficacy in science were significant predictors of the career options actually considered, over and above abilities and interest, thus validating theoretical relationships between efficacy and choice behavior (Betz & Hackett, 1981).

In another series of studies, we measured math self-efficacy, or students' beliefs about their competence to perform math tasks and problems and to get adequate grades in math courses (Betz & Hackett, 1983). Not only did we find the predictable and large gender differences, with males being much more self-efficacious with respect to math than females, but we found that math self-efficacy was related to the science relatedness of college major choice (along with math background and math ACT). Low math and science self-efficacy led to a reduction in the options a person would even consider.

One interesting side finding was that if we asked the right questions, we found women were as self-efficacious as men when it came to math. Table 4.3 shows a few of the items in the measure of math self-efficacy—everyday math tasks. Students just had to say how competent they felt that they could successfully engage in a given task. Note that overall, there were 52 math self-efficacy items. The 3 items with asterisks indicate where females scored higher than males on self-efficacy: figuring out how much material to buy to make curtains, estimating your grocery bill in your head as you pick up items, and calculating recipes. Note the female-stereotypic content of these items—implying that if test items and math problems are developed that use content more familiar to the socialization backgrounds of females than males (in contrast to the male-oriented content usually used), females might perform better than they do on the standard male-oriented content. I am not suggesting that we should make sure girls know how to sew, shop for groceries, and cook! But their back-

---

Table 4.3 Illustrative Items From the Mathematics Self-Efficacy Scale

---

Math tasks: How much confidence do you have that you could successfully

  figure out how much lumber you need to buy in order to build a set of bookshelves?
  figure out how much material to buy in order to make curtains?[a]
  compute your car's gas mileage?
  set up a monthly budget for yourself?
  balance your checkbook without a mistake?
  estimate your grocery bill in your head as you pick up items?[a]
  calculate recipe quantities for a dinner for 4 when the original recipe is for 12 people?[a]
  determine the amount of sales tax on a clothing purchase?

SOURCE: Adapted from Betz and Hackett (1983).
NOTE: Of 52 math self-efficacy items, males reported significantly higher expectation of efficacy on 24 items and higher expectations on 25 more, or a total of 49 of 52.
a. The three items on which females scored higher.

---

ground experiences often make those content domains more familiar to them. So when questions are asked the right way to a measure of this type—and this applies to both test content and course content—all of a sudden, girls seem to feel better about their competence to do math. This has some implications. Keep self-efficacy in mind. It is important in understanding retention as well as choices. Also, the four sources of efficacy information can be used as the basis for the design of intervention programs.

Even if you perceive it as okay for you as a girl or a Black or a Hispanic to do science, and even if you think you are competent enough to do it, you must also perceive yourself as having interests in the area—that it would be fun to do. One of the most disturbing patterns in research on vocational interests is that women and U.S. minority members tend to score highly on measures of social interests and much lower in scientific and technical areas. In essence, we are teaching women and minority students that they are good at helping people but not good at occupations where they have to think. I believe interests are changeable throughout life. All of us develop interests as we grow older. I am not willing to think that interests are fully developed by the time one goes to college. One area of interest at this point that I am pursuing is the nature of interest development, how we develop our vocational interests in the first place. Second, I am studying the modifiability of that development. I see no reason why we cannot assist more women and minority people to develop strong vocational interests in the sciences.

Influences on the Development of Career Interests

Of the women who took one well-known interest inventory, 67% were classified as social (Prediger & Hanson, 1976). Only 8% came out highest on scientific (investigative) and 1% on technical (realistic). It is only a slight exaggeration to say that the best predictor of a person's interests is gender—a violation of the valued concept of individual differences in psychological traits. We know that there is no basis to assume that gender differences in interests have a biological basis, for at least two reasons: (a) Black males tend to show the same socially oriented patterns of interests as do both White and Black females and (b) Asian females show a degree of interest in science and abilities comparable to that of White males. Thus, there is much evidence for the basis of interests to be in gender role and cultural socialization rather than genetics. We are doing a good job of socializing scientific interests in White boys but not in girls, with the exception of Asian girls, and not in minority boys. We are teaching non-Asian minorities that they can be successful in careers where they can help people (e.g., teaching, social work) but not in careers where their major job is to think. We need much more research on the development of interests in science and, in my opinion, should work on the assumption that new interests can be developed throughout one's life, most certainly in college.

To summarize at this point, we need more research enabling us to understand and modify positively at least three areas of maladaptive cognitions: (a) stereotypes regarding science and scientists, (b) low science and math self-efficacy expectations, and (c) lack of interests in science. It also goes without saying that efforts in the secondary schools to keep young women and minority students in math and science through 12th grade and to encourage minority students to follow college prep curricula are imperative.

Ways to Make Changes

Improved Guidance Counseling, More Outreach Programs

One important avenue of change lies within the field of science education and guidance counseling at the elementary and secondary levels. But because my focus here is higher education, I would also suggest that a much-needed avenue involves outreach programs to high school students from colleges and universities. We need many more such programs. An excellent example of such a program is the Women in Science Program at the University of Michigan, a program of summer internships in science for high school women. The model program involved the cooperation of women scientists and engineers from both academic and industrial settings. Each student selected (from among high school women who had obtained grades of B or better in math and science courses) spent 30 hours a week for 6 weeks working on a research project under the mentorship of a woman scientist or engineer. In addition, the program involved weekly lunch meetings with program participants and women scientists from other fields so that students could get a broader look at careers in the sciences. The summer ended with a public Student Science Symposium. The students then returned for their senior year of high school and agreed to do workshops and presentations with younger women students so that they too could act as role models. Consider the benefits if many more colleges and universities could support programs of this nature for both women and minority students. Initial funding for program development could come from federal, state, or university sources, or a combination of these, with subsequent support from the local businesses and industries that will stand to gain in the long run.

Counterstereotypical Role Models

Other programs could focus on bringing adult minority and women scientists and engineers into the secondary schools to provide role modeling and information functions but also to challenge stereotypes of scientists. For example, an athletic, stylishly dressed young Black scientist and an engineer who was also married and a mother are among the kinds of role models that might be useful. Films, videos, and changes in the media might also be very helpful. For instance, the effectiveness of films, videos, and public service ads featuring women and minority scientists should be studied.

Better Understanding of the Formation of Interests Is Needed

We also need to know more about the development of interests in science and math. We are currently beginning studies of the relationship to interests in science of both science-related self-efficacy expectations and stereotypes of scientists. I postulate that the more competent you feel in a domain of behavior, the more likely you are to express and pursue interests in it. There is also reason to postulate that negative stereotypes may lead to a reduced degree of cognitive processing of information. If this decline of information could be reversed, the result could be increased interest in the area on the part of girls or minority students. If either of these postulates is supported by research, the findings would point the way to interventions that could increase interest in science among young women and minority group members.

Don't Give Up on Interest Formation Just Because the Student Is in College

Another important point of focus for intervention involves students just beginning college work. We need to make the assumption that it is not too late to encourage students to consider science and engineering majors—even in their freshman and sophomore years of college—and develop research and intervention programs that could assist in this process. We know that 20% of science and engineering majors did not enter college planning to be majors in those areas. Rather, they selected science and engineering as freshmen or sophomores. There is always a large pool of undecided students, some of whom have enough ability to pursue science. There is also a pool of potential teachers who may be swayed—by good teaching and advising in addition to support—to consider specializing in high school math and science, including computer science. I say this not only because we need more secondary school math and science teachers but also because getting more minority people and women to teach high school math and science will add to the presence of role models and the overall lessening of stereotypes. Ninety-three percent of math and science teachers are White.

Once the Student Is Committed, See That the Commitment Is Supported

Once we get young people to choose science majors, we need to ensure that more of the academically able, interested ones are able to complete their degrees. With minority students, retention in undergraduate and graduate programs is a problem so serious that most researchers in this area deem it of major crisis proportions. For example, if we define college completion as the attainment of a baccalaureate degree within 6 years of starting it, we find that about one half of Whites but only one fourth of Blacks and Hispanics complete their degrees. Eventually, 77% of Whites and 45% of Blacks and Hispanics do finish. To look at this another way, about 70% of Black, Hispanic, and Native American students who started college between 1980 and 1982 had dropped out by 1986 versus about 50% of Whites and Asians. In science, retention of minority students is even worse. We lose twice as many Black as White science and engineering majors. The attrition of minority students has to do with poor academic preparation, inadequate financial resources, and, in White-dominated universities, the perceived inhospitality of the environment in combination with a relative lack of social support for their aspirations.

Whereas we lose minority students at both the undergraduate and graduate level, we tend to lose women in graduate school, especially after the master's degree. Table 4.4 illustrates this rather dramatically. You'll note the percentage of degrees earned by women goes down as the educational level goes up. Because women entering graduate programs are about as well prepared academically as are the men, we again look to the institutional climate and the lack of social support to explain the losses we incur in the production of female doctorates in the sciences.

Clearly, discrimination is alive and well in higher education. Research on the institutional climate has documented not only overt discrimination, such as higher admissions requirements for female than male applicants, sex quotas for admission, discrimination in the award of financial aid, and sexual harassment, but more subtle forms as well.

Table 4.4 Proportions of Science and Engineering Degrees Awarded to Women Across Fields and Degree Levels

Field	BS	MS	PhD
Sciences	45.3	40.5	31.7
Physical	29.7	24.9	16.8
Mathematical	46.5	35.2	16.2
Computer	35.8	29.9	10.9
Environmental	22.3	23.1	19.8
Life	44.0	41.4	32.9
Psychology	69.0	64.9	54.8
Social	43.4	3.9	33.1
Engineering	14.5	11.6	6.8
Aeronautical-astronautical	8.5	6.9	6.0
Chemical	24.7	15.7	9.6
Civil	13.1	10.2	5.1
Electrical	12.0	10.0	4.3
Industrial	30.1	16.9	15.0
Mechanical	10.3	7.7	4.3
Other	16.8	13.7	8.4

SOURCE: Adapted from NSF (1990)
NOTE: Proportions reflect BS and PhD degrees earned in 1988 and MS degrees earned in 1986.

More subtle forms of discrimination are reflected in behaviors leading to the avoidance of, failure to support, or active disparagement of women and minority students, or combinations of these. A few examples are (a) disparaging women's and minority students' intellectual capabilities or professional potential; (b) ridiculing or trivializing their questions in class or, alternatively, ignoring their attempts to participate; (c) advising them to lower their academic and career goals, in other words, downscaling; (d) responding with surprise when they express demanding career goals; (e) not actively encouraging them to apply for fellowships, grants, and awards; and (f) focusing on marital and parental status as a potential barrier to the career development of women but as an advantage for men.

Even if such discrimination isn't occurring, the environment may be nonsupportive both in actuality and psychologically. First, most faculty role models in the sciences and engineering continue to be

White men. And whereas we know that most women scientists and engineers report male models and mentors, these women were the ones who succeeded. We need to know more about the women and minority students who didn't make it, not just about those who did. We do know that the quality of the advising in graduate schools in science and engineering is crucial to career development for both development of research interests and competencies and for informal socialization and networking as well.

Women graduate students at Stanford (Zappert & Stansbury, 1984) reported two difficult battles. The first was convincing a faculty member to become their mentor. The second was maintaining the close working relationship with the mentor that is necessary to turn a graduate student into an independent scientist and scholar. The fact is that most science and engineering professors are male, and whether it is a conscious process or not, most male professors are more comfortable with and accustomed to male students.

Rosabeth Kanter's (1977) research suggests that numerical minorities in work organizations tend to be excluded from informal and discretionary interactions, even if it is not done consciously. In graduate school, discretionary approaches from a faculty member include inviting the students to work on his or her research, either voluntarily or as a paid research assistant, to coauthor a paper, and to present together at a scientific meeting. Informal interactions include having lunch together, participating in sports (such as golf or the department's intramural basketball team), and being introduced by him or her to colleagues attending conventions. These typically have been interactions that have favored White males and left out minority members or females.

Other problems face "token" women and minority people. First, it may be hard to feel that you belong there when nobody else looks like you. The flip side to the fact that nobody else looks like you is that you stick out like a sore thumb. For most of us, this kind of visibility conveys a vulnerability that can impede behavior and undermine self-confidence. Tokens may also feel (often justifiably) that their performance will reflect well or poorly on their entire sex or race. And sometimes it does, if it is interpreted in a sexist or racist fashion. Again, the resulting anxiety and perfectionism can be debilitating to performance.

Last, being a token is just plain lonely. For women or minority group members in science and engineering, the most important ingredient becomes the presence of other women or minority students and faculty. Ehrhart and Sandler (1987) have termed this the *comfort factor*, and other researchers have called this a *critical mass*. Researchers have postulated that the lack of a critical mass continues to constitute a serious barrier to retention. When the critical mass is reached, there are sufficient opportunities for social support, and the feeling that "there are others in the same boat" can encourage a woman or minority person to persist. We also need to get more of these students to pursue academic careers so that the composition of faculties, as well as of student bodies, will gradually lose their homogeneous quality. That alone may considerably increase retention.

A High Expectation of Efficacy Is a Crucial Factor in Retention and Success

Given an environment characterized by discrimination, whether overt or subtle, and a relative lack of support, other environmental and personal factors may become crucial determinants to survival and persistence in demanding educational programs. Again, one of the personal qualities that I have focused on is that of self-efficacy, which is postulated to affect not only choice but persistence. The better you feel about your competence, the more it is postulated that you will stick in a situation when the going gets tough—much longer than you would if you didn't feel very confident about your abilities. And although college programs are demanding for White males as well as for females and minority members, research suggests that White males do have more of the kind of familial and peer, not to mention societal, support for their educational and career goals than do women or minority students. Thus, personal resources may become a key to survival. I have focused my research on the cognitive mediational factors that enable a student to survive and persist in a nonsupportive educational environment. Specifically, we have postulated that strong science-math self-efficacy expectations are related not only to the initial choice of a science-engineering major, but to performance and persistence once you get there.

First of all, we do have evidence that women generally have lower expectations of efficacy with respect to completing science and engineering majors than do comparably able men. This is even true among students actually majoring in science and engineering. We have looked at two basic subject populations: engineering students at the University of California at Santa Barbara and students in the Institute of Technology at the University of Minnesota.

Hackett and I and our colleagues studied 220 high-ability students in the School of Engineering at the University of California at Santa Barbara and found that the women students reported significantly lower expectations of self-efficacy than did the men in relationship to the steps necessary to get an engineering degree (Hackett, Betz, Cases, & Rocha-Singh, 1992). Differences in self-efficacy occurred in spite of equivalent high school grades, SATs, and measured interests in the sciences and engineering. The women still felt less self-efficacious. We further found that self-efficacy was a significant predictor of first-year grades. We also had a large sample of Hispanic students, and they, too, had significantly lower self-efficacy expectations with respect to their degree work than did White males. Again, we found that self-efficacy was a significant predictor of performance.

At the University of Minnesota, Lent, Brown, and Larkin (1984, 1986) found clear evidence that high self-efficacy is a significant predictor of persistence in those majors one year later, over and above the effects of measured ability. College students in the Institute of Technology were divided into high self-efficacy and low self-efficacy groups. Of the former, 100% stayed enrolled all four quarters following the study, whereas only about 50% of the latter persisted that long. Note that these were *all* high-ability students, as they had been admitted to the well-regarded Institute of Technology at the University of Minnesota. In subsequent studies of this population at Minnesota, self-efficacy of high-ability science and engineering majors contributed unique variance to the prediction of grades and persistence in science and engineering majors over and above the effects of ability.

One implication, then, of this research, is that programs of intervention designed to increase a student's expectations of self-efficacy are potentially valuable. What this particular series of studies suggests is that the strengthening of individual self-confidence concerning the pursuit of a science and engineering degree may be an important buffer to the lack of support or, worse, overt discrimination. Thus, our interventions regarding retention should be directed at both helping individuals and improving the institutional climate.

Table 4.5 summarizes some general possibilities for the retention of women and minority students. I have compiled many of these from other materials. It is important to intervene both at the level of individuals and of organizations. We need to help individuals develop resources to get them through school, but we also need gradually to make environments more hospitable to women and minority students. You will note there are many individual support possibilities that could be tried. This is not to say that all have been proven effective in keeping women and minority students in the sciences, but they are definitely potentially important components of programs.

Considerations for Future Research

We need more and better data collection about retention, especially at the graduate level, and disaggregated by gender and minority status. We need disaggregation especially so that we can see what is happening to minority women. Minority women suffer from two forms of suppression by society, being female and being members of a minority. We need to know more about what is happening to them, and the only way we can see that is if the data are disaggregated.

Another characteristic of retention research is that it is not always easy to know who is and who is not still a graduate student. The average time from baccalaureate to doctorate has been steadily increasing. It is now 10.5 years. Such long times to degree make it hard to know who has dropped out versus who is just "taking a break." If we could identify the dropouts, we could conduct exit interviews to determine what the reasons were for leaving, and what environmental or personal changes could have made the difference between retention versus loss of a gifted woman or minority student. Research on the concept of the critical mass would help now. Clearly, research of this kind could help us set priorities as far as interventions within higher educational institutions. An exit interview could be highly informative. Thus, research in this area should receive highest priority.

Table 4.5   Interventions for Increasing the Retention of Women
and Minority Science and Engineering Students

Individual Support

Summer orientation programs prior to entrance, especially for minorities

Academic support programs, especially for minorities (e.g., tutoring, study table, first-year classes taught by informed or minority instructors, or both)

Social support

> Student organizations (e.g., Society for Women Engineers, Black Graduate
> Student Association)
>
> Counseling or support groups offered by counseling centers or, even better,
> science departments
>
> Resident hall floors for special groups
>
> Personal support, that is, facilitating development of strong beliefs in self
> (e.g., using self-efficacy theory as a model of the strengthening of science-
> engineering self-efficacy)
>
> Financial support, especially a focus on increasing the number of research
> assistantships at both undergraduate and graduate levels

Increasing perceptions of job-relatedness (e.g., science and engineering-related co-op programs, summer internships in industry or summer research internships)

Recruitment for graduate study, especially with minorities

> Active solicitation (e.g., recruiting trips to Black colleges or to schools with large
> minority enrollments)
>
> Information to students about graduate school opportunities and the application
> process
>
> Faculty support for, and encouragement of, talented women and minority stu-
> dents toward graduate school aspirations
>
> Minority visitation days, especially including visits to science and engineering
> departments.

Institutional Change

Increase the number of women and minority professors.

Increase the sensitivity of the well-represented groups (the insiders) to the needs of those who feel like outsiders—such change should focus on faculty, administration, and "majority" students.

Convince faculty that no type of discrimination, whether overt or subtle, is acceptable.

Reward departments that increase their critical mass of underrepresented groups.

Work toward increasing the critical mass with the idea that numeric sufficiency of women and minorities will eventually provide a natural support system and allevia-tion of some of the problems caused by inhospitable environments.

Another focus of research should be experimental and quasi-experimental studies of the effectiveness of different components of interventions, for example, role modeling, support systems, academic support, financial aid, and counseling aimed at increasing personal efficacy and self-esteem. Funding of model programs that are carefully evaluated should be a major current focus of federal and private funding efforts.

Some Policy Recommendations

First, there is some federal and foundation funding available right now to increase the quality of scientific education in general and to get more women and minority members into the sciences in particular. But I think much more needs to be done. It is simply too important an issue, and too serious an issue, to not put a lot more money into it.

Second, more money for the evaluation of model programs for recruitment and retention of women and minority members is needed. And more money for basic research on the psychological factors related to choosing and persisting in science and engineering majors is necessary, especially because such research can help us design potentially effective interventions.

Third, universities and business could be stimulated to do much more. Institutions of higher education have been putting increasing resources into minority recruitment and retention, but these interventions have not usually been targeted toward the sciences per se. And industry should play a much more aggressive and proactive role because they stand to benefit at a level greater than the money they would need to put into it. Public dollars spent on education in general and on increasing the pool of women and minority scientists and engineers in particular seem to me to have the potential to benefit society at a level much greater than the original dollar amount. I do not need to convince you of the myriad ways in which this country's collective productivity and individual quality of life are dependent on scientific advances and technical skill and ingenuity.

Fourth, we need to convince more policymakers and the public of the potentially great effects of developing rather than wasting a large segment of our scientific and technical talent. Given attention now, some of these problems could be greatly alleviated. As more women and minority members pursue the sciences and engineering, more teachers from these groups should be visible at the secondary school, college, and university levels. Their presence should make the educational environment appear a friendlier place to a young woman or minority student, a place where such young persons could feel a sense of belonging. Thus, as the number of these professionals increases, it may become easier to attract and retain other women and minority students.

What Specifically Can the Federal Government Do Regarding Science and Engineering?

Let me count the ways:

1. Sustain academic research and development funding.
2. Expand graduate and postdoctoral traineeships and fellowships.
3. Support institutions that make special contributions to undergraduate science and engineering education (historically Black colleges and universities, women's colleges, and primarily engineering institutions).
4. Target financial support for undergraduate science and engineering students.
5. Strengthen NSF leadership in science and engineering education, and enlarge Department of Education contributions.
6. Support research and intervention programs targeted toward individual support and institutional change.

In summary, there is clearly a need to encourage more women and non-Asian minority members to choose and stay in educational programs in the sciences and engineering, from undergraduate through doctorate degrees. Special attention should be focused on programs in the physical sciences and engineering, the two areas particularly underrepresented, and intervention efforts should be focused on both choice issues and retention issues in higher education. I would urge our attention to this effort. Thank you for beginning a personal effort by taking the time to read these pages thoughtfully.

———•◆•————•◆•————•◆•———

Q: *What can parents of girls and minority members do to encourage their children to go into (and stay in) science and engineering?*

A: I don't know of any particular studies of that nature. The work I do know of is more of the specific outreach programs to elementary and particularly secondary school students to get them involved in science internship programs and related hands-on activities. You can involve your child in science at home. Give your kid a chemistry set!

Q: *Has anyone thought of having a college devoted to science and math exclusively for women?*

A: Women's colleges disproportionately produce scientists. They are very good. So are Black universities. There should be more support for 4-year colleges that are very strongly oriented towards science and engineering. So much federal support goes to graduate institutions instead of undergraduate institutions that are dedicated to science and engineering education. Women and minority students in particular ought to be highlighted, targeted, and funded. I would suggest that alternative. But a women's college is a great place to find budding young women engineers and scientists.

Q: *To follow up, there have been some data presented that private schools are better at retaining women and minority students in science majors. I would assume it is probably a more supportive environment, generally speaking, than a large, 4-year public institution. Would you like to talk a little about that?*

A: I have also read that data. I think an institution without a graduate program tends to do a lot more for undergraduate students. One of my recommendations for the federal government is to provide much more undergraduate support. Let's get undergraduates doing research while they are undergraduates. Too often in a graduate institution, the graduate students get all the research assistantships. This is great because they need them, but more money could be profitably directed toward undergraduate institutions.

Q: *Research money has gone from high to low. There is no point in going into science if there is no career. Too often we worry about money for training. But if there is nothing out there when you get through, then what is the point?*

A: You're right. There should be more financial aid for women and minority students, perhaps targeted for women and minority people who will pursue sciences versus generic, broad financial aid. But there indeed also needs to be money to do research afterwards.

Q: *Some data suggest that at some critical point in the early school years, a lot of kids choose not to choose science, both male and female. Isn't there a need to look at that?*

A: You are suggesting that much of the loss of interest in science occurs at the middle school level. That is not an area in which I am an expert. Jackie Eccles, who I understand is also participating in this series, is an expert in that area, and I would recommend that you take a look at what she has to say.

Q: *I think socialization starts as soon as children are born. Kids who are 2 and 3 years old are being socialized, particularly minority children, about school and science. This country socializes in a way that is a disadvantage to minority members. Blacks and Hispanics may be socialized differently. What is being done on the early elementary level? Many minority students never make it to college at all. What you are talking about may perhaps be too late and is a symbol of a bigger problem.*

A: I did not specialize in child development, so I cannot speak knowledgeably about this. I think we need a lot more researchers working on this problem at different levels. But just as I mentioned that Jackie Eccles has specialized in the middle school years, Diana Slaughter-Defoe, who is part of this series, has specialized in home effects on schooling, and Janet Schofield has specialized in the socialization process for African American students in segregated and desegregated schools at the elementary and secondary levels. I suggest you take a look at their work.

Q: *Are there any efforts to promote areas in the private sector involving such things as reclamation and hazardous waste where students could possibly use a biology degree, undergraduate or master's, and actually enter the area of science and engineering without necessarily obtaining a doctorate? We only need so many high-level scientists, but we do need technicians, and so forth. We could perhaps get people into these tracks where they can do the support work as well as some challenging work. This is an avenue a lot of minority members and women could pursue. The whole idea of being a scientist is a great idea for some people, but it might not be for everyone. They should be getting in the area where they can use their talents but perhaps not at the doctorate level. The private sector could promote this.*

A: Your point reminds me of the fact that 11% of scientists and engineers hold doctorates and 89% do not. So my emphasis on the doctorate is somewhat misplaced because the large majority of scientists and engineers have bachelor's or master's degrees, particularly in engineering. So you are exactly right. Our efforts in retaining students through undergraduate degrees in science and engineering are in some sense even more crucial than the push to generate new doctorate holders. I would also suggest more business and industry involvement. They stand to gain, and they should pay.

Q: *How do you open up this dialogue with business and industry and make them aware of this? It is, after all, in their best interest. My boss here in Congress has been trying to get the private sector to sit down with NASA, just to sit across the table and say, "You need workers, and we have kids coming out of school. What can we do to help each other?"*

A: I would ask other successful programs how they manage to get corporations to support their programs financially.

Q: *The congressional committee I work for has been very concerned about how much NSF is doing to address all the issues raised here today, not just retaining through high school and college women and minority students who are already interested in science and mathematics but also attracting women and minority members at a younger age. Do you know how much NSF is really doing? They talk a lot about it. How successful have they been?*

A: There are preschool and day care science programs that are representative of early efforts to influence initial choices. There are some science museums around the country that are opening their doors to Head Start groups. A lot is beginning to be done there. But I don't think much is being done at the college level, and much more needs to be done.

Audience Member: I work at NSF; let me respond. The precollege area takes up about 50% of NSF's science education budget. That's around $200 million. Obviously, that is not enough money to do the job that needs to be done. Also, science education is not exactly isolated in the education scheme of things, so NSF is not really the only player. There are a number of very excellent programs.

Q: *It is not just the level of funding. I have to look at some of these grant proposals, and a lot of them involve some faculty member who wants to run some little special program in the summer. So they run it, and whoever comes, comes. Efforts need to be made to make sure that some of the people participating are girls and minority students.*

A: In addition, I would say it is imperative that the little program in the summer be evaluated. If it is good, it should be disseminated. I have seen too many of these little programs in the summer die right there, and that is the last we ever hear of them.

Q: *I have a question about minority faculty members. At the present time, there aren't many minorities or women coming out of college with advanced degrees. Do you propose giving them time to work their way up or massively recruiting them and then hoping for the best? It seems like an insoluble problem because you can't get to where you want to be because to get there, you have to have it already.*

A: There aren't enough minority and women doctorates coming out. I think it certainly might help get more women and minority faculty if, in graduate school, more of them have funded research assistantships and are actively involved in research and strongly oriented toward academic careers. It is a very serious problem. They have to want to be researchers and academics.

Q: *I have been one of those trying to get a science degree, going through a large, predominantly White school and being told, "I don't have time right now. Come back and see me later." There is more concentration on students who are doing well, and the students who need the help get pushed aside. My question is directed at the gentleman from NSF who could probably help me a little bit. Of the programs you say you have money for, how many really get into the neighborhoods that need them? I come from the inner city. When I was growing up, I did not see these programs.*

A: *Audience Member:* I don't make a really good representative of the Education and Human Resources Directorate at NSF because I am not part of it, but let me say there are a whole host of programs that deal with high school students, teacher training and preparation, and even getting junior high kids and high school teachers into laboratories in the summers. In 1981, funding was cut from NSF for science education. What essentially dried up was all the high school teacher training and all the young scholars and minority scholars programs. Now, with everyone taking renewed interest in these programs, they are back in full swing. I can't really speak to the details of which cities, and so forth, but you would be surprised now if you looked at the array of programs that are in place at the NSF. You would not, however, be impressed with the number of dollars there are for each program. That is what would scare you.

Senator Glenn had a hearing yesterday morning at which it was stated that the federal effort for science and math education was about a billion dollars, a couple hundred million from NSF, and assorted amounts from each of the major agencies. By the way, 4-H is one of the big science education programs funded by the federal government. That is the one that touches

136

millions of kids. All the others touch 50 or 100 kids at a time. Anyhow, a billion dollars was quoted. People seemed impressed, but that's 20 bucks a kid! So maybe you did see some of those programs. If you got a textbook, that is your share. A billion dollars doesn't go very far when you have 40 or 50 million kids. It costs about a billion dollars a year to run science and math teachers through a summer institute, and that's a billion dollars a year forever because they need to do it every 5 or 10 years, and there are a half million of them in need of the service. In addition, teachers can't work while in the institutes, so we really should pay them. If you want to replace the science instrumentation (K-12), you are also talking billions of dollars. You'll want to continue that effort every 5 or 10 years before it is obsolete again, so that's also billions of dollars forever. You very quickly come to a shortfall before you talk about computers, changing teachers colleges, scholarships, and fellowships. If you then seriously want to expand into some of the stuff we have been talking about here, which would work, it gets to be very large numbers. So NSF may be faulted for not using its money well, but we don't know that. They don't have much money. It is really hard to see the outcome. The input is very small, so it is no surprise the outcome is small.

Q: *You noted the high proportion of Asian minorities in science fields. I wonder what reasons you might have as to why they are so well represented. Why doesn't this provide us with ideas for programs?*

A: I am glad you asked that question. Americans are among the few who attribute math performance to something genetic! Asians attribute it to hard work. Work hard and you will make something successful of yourself. I don't want to generalize because there are many Asian cultures, but let's say Japanese, Chinese, and Korean cultures. There is a cultural ethic of hard work—that is, study hard, get all the education you can. They don't talk about an Asian gene for math ability. They talk about hard work and appropriate study. And I think that is what we can learn. We don't have to sit around and talk about whether women and minority members are genetically less able to do math. Rather, I like what Alexander Astin (1982) calls the talent development point of view. Let's take students where they are and help develop their talents. There are excellent programs right now at Berkeley and other universities for mathematics talent development in Black students, which suggests that if Black students with the lowest Scholastic Assessment Tests (SAT) scores are given strong remedial treatment their first year in college, they can perform better in calculus courses than students with much higher SATs. I like the talent development point of view, and I think that would be my answer to why Asians are so well represented among our scientists and engineers. Of course, recent court decisions and recent political sentiment against programs that take positive steps to bring minority students to college and keep them there through graduation may be devastating for these efforts. Time will tell, but at this point, these legal and political decisions seem to be a very unfortunate blow to some critical programs.

Q: *Elementary school teachers are generally not science majors. Even in high school, the science teachers are usually not scientists. Is there anything going on in the education departments to improve this? These teachers usually do not like teaching science and math.*

A: That brings up all sorts of additional issues. We did some math anxiety treatment groups for Ohio State University students, and we found that the most math-anxious students on campus were the elementary education students. They were terrified, and, of course, that is communicated to children. My bias is that more education aspirants should actually have majors in science. Then, their pedagogical training becomes an asset that they can apply to their substantive knowledge of science and math.

There is a team-teaching concept that is now developing. Scientists who work in the area can come into the K-12 classrooms and work with students. These scientists are very confident of their abilities. This concept does not require putting a lot of money into raising the comfort level, if you will, of teachers—so they will feel like they can do math and science.

Some other studies have shown that if you look at the grades K-6, science and math are normally taught the last period of the day, for about the last 15 minutes of the day. Everyone is getting ready to go home. Everyone is tired. And if there is a class picnic or assembly, forget it! So, as I say, the issue of how to teach teachers to teach science opens a great many issues that are fully worthy of exploration in their own forum. Thank you again for your thoughtful attention to what I and the other researchers in this series have shared with you.

•◆••◆••◆•

References

Astin, A. (1982). *Minorities in higher education*. San Francisco: Jossey-Bass.

Bandura, A. (1977). Self-efficacy: Toward a unifying theory of behavioral change. *Psychological Review, 84*, 191-215.

Benbow, C. P. (1988). Sex differences in mathematical reasoning ability in intellectually talented preadolescents: Their nature, effects and possible causes. *Behavioral and Brain Sciences, 11*, 169-183, 217-232.

Betz, N. E., & Hackett, G. (1981). The relationship of career-related self-efficacy expectations to perceived career options in college women and men. *Journal of Counseling Psychology, 28*, 339-410.

Betz, N. E., & Hackett, G. (1983). The relationship of mathematics self-efficacy expectations to the selection of science-based college majors. *Journal of Vocational Behavior, 23*, 329-345.

Drabman, R. S., Robertson, S. J., Patterson, J. N., Jarvie, G. J., Hammer, D., & Cordua, G. (1981). Children's perception of media portrayed sex roles. *Sex Roles, 7*, 379-390.

Ehrhart, J. K., & Sandler, B. R. (1987). *Looking for more than a few good women in traditionally male fields*. Washington, DC: American Association of Colleges, Project on the Status and Education of Women.

Green, K. C. (1989). A profile of undergraduates in the sciences. *American Scientist, 7*, 475-480.

Hackett, G., & Betz, N. E. (1981). A self-efficacy approach to the career development of women. *Journal of Vocational Behavior, 18*, 326-339.

Hackett, G., Betz, N., Cases, J. M., & Rocha-Singh, I. A. (1992). Gender, ethnicity, and social cognitive factors predicting the academic achievement of students in engineering. *Journal of Counseling Psychology, 39*, 527-538.

Kanter, R. (1977). *Men and women of the corporation*. New York: Basic Books.

Lent, R. W., Brown, S. D., & Larkin, K. C. (1984). Relation of self-efficacy expectations to academic achievement and persistence. *Journal of Counseling Psychology, 31*, 356-362.

Lent, R. W., Brown, S. D., & Larkin, K. C. (1986). Self-efficacy in the prediction of academic success and perceived career options. *Journal of Counseling Psychology, 33*, 265-269.

Lubinsky, D., & Humphreys, L. G. (1990). A broadly based analysis of mathematical giftedness. *Intelligence, 14*, 327-356.

Mead, M., & Metraux, R. (1957). Images of the scientists among high school students. *Science, 126*, 384-390.

National Science Board. (1996). *Science and engineering indicators.* Washington, DC: Government Printing Office.

National Science Foundation. (1990). *Women and minorities in science and engineering.* Washington, DC: Government Printing Office.

Pietrofessa, J. J., & Schlossberg, N. K. (1970). *Counselor bias and the female occupational role.* (ERIC Document No. CG 006 056)

Prediger, D. P., & Hanson, G. R. (1976). Holland's theory of careers applied to men and women: An analysis of implicit assumptions. *Journal of Vocational Behavior, 8,* 157-164.

Sells, L. (1982). Leverage for equal opportunity through mastery of mathematics. In S. M. Humphreys (Ed.), *Women and minorities in science* (pp. 7-26). Boulder, CO: Westview.

Why do so few students want to become scientists? (1988). *Harvard Education Letter, 4,* p. 6.

Zappert, L., & Stansbury, K. (1984). *In the pipeline: A comparative analysis of men and women in graduate programs in science, engineering, and medicine at Stanford University.* Stanford, CA: Stanford University.

Index

About the Editor

———•◆•———

David Johnson is Executive Director of the Federation of Behavioral, Psychological and Cognitive Sciences, a coalition of scientific societies. The Federation, based in Washington, D.C., represents the legislative and regulatory interests of behavioral researchers, educates lawmakers and federal officials about behavioral research and its relevance to matters of public policy, and keeps scientists informed of Washington developments that could affect research and teaching.

After receiving his doctorate in social psychology from Stanford University in 1980, he became a fellow of the Duke University Round Table on Science and Public Affairs. He worked as the aide to the chairman of the Education Appropriations Committee and as a staff member of Governor Jim Hunt's Science and Commerce Advisory Committee. After a year in state government, he went to Washington where he began the second half of his fellowship as a legislative assistant on matters of science and education for then-Congressman Mervyn M. Dymally, a representative from Southern California and a member of the House Committee on Science and Technology. He became Dymally's administrative assistant, a post in which he served for 6 years. Among his duties was to be executive director of the Congressional Caucus for Science and Technology, an organization of representatives and senators interested in advancing science through legislation. He left Dymally's staff in 1987 to become Director of the Federation. He writes regularly on science and public policy.

About the Authors

———————— •◆• ————————

Nancy Betz is Full Professor in Ohio State University's Department of Psychology. She received her doctorate in counseling psychology from the University of Minnesota in 1976. In her research, she has paid special attention to understanding the factors that limit the choices of women and minorities, especially those that limit their ability to enter careers in science and technology. She deals with the consequences of our elementary and secondary education systems—the students who enter college and succeed, those who enter and struggle, and those unable to enter or complete college. She has focused on students whose educational experience prior to college puts them at risk of not completing college study or artificially limits the choices they can make for majors, graduate study, and careers. Women and members of minority groups have long been underrepresented in most fields of science and engineering.

In her professional work, Betz applies what she has learned to expanding the choices effectively available to college students. In her own university, for example, she has worked on the Provost's Committee for the Retention of Academically At-Risk Students, chairing the subcomittee responsible for defining the conditions that identify a student as being at risk. She lectures on factors affecting the performance and choices of women and minorities in universities, including the impact of math anxiety on women's performance and the role of one's personal beliefs about self-competence and self-efficacy on one's decision to perfect skills required of particular careers.

Jacquelynne Eccles is a professor and senior scientist at the University of Michigan. The question that motivates her research is this: Given similar abilities, why is there a great disparity in learning and performance between one person and another, one group and another? Learning occurs in a social context that provides or withholds motivation to learn and perform. It also tells a person (rightly or wrongly) about his or her abilities. A self-perception emerges that aids or impedes further learning and performance that colors one's interpretation of new information. Social context provides very different cues about learning and ability to boys than to girls, to White students than to Black students. It should be possible to arrange environments to bring out the best in all students. Eccles works to understand positive and negative environments and to create optimal learning environments. It is evident that the middle school environment is especially critical, giving some students the boost that propels them into college and proving intensely discouraging to others. Thus, she has paid particular attention to middle school.

Eccles uses the knowledge she has gained to help steer public policies and programs in productive directions. She has chaired the National Science Foundation's Committee on Equal Opportunity in Science, Engineering and Technology and the Advisory Committee for NSF's Directorate for Social, Behavioral and Economic Sciences. She has been a member of the Carnegie Council on Adolescent Development Task Force on Education for the Middle Grades and the MacArthur Foundation Network on Adolescent Development in Risky Environments.

Janet Ward Schofield is Full Professor of psychology and senior scientist at the University of Pittsburgh's Learning Research and Development Center. Through the 1970s and early 1980s, her research on desegregation provided some of the most detailed knowledge available on the varieties of desegregation and the varying effects it can have on students.

Commitment to using research to help children learn came early to her. While completing her doctorate in social psychology at Harvard in 1969, she taught psychology and sociology at Atlanta's Spelman College. There, she saw brilliant African American students putting substantial effort into overcoming impediments from their prior educations. From Spelman, she went as a research psychologist to the

Policy Research Division of the Office of Economic Opportunity and then to the National Institute of Education in Washington, D.C. Those experiences showed her how public policies can facilitate or discourage learning, how policies can implement either sound, science-based practices or those with no empirical grounding. These encounters shaped an action-oriented career. In recent years, she and her colleagues have embarked on a grand experiment with the National Science Foundation and Pittsburgh schools—an effort to use research in the schools themselves to improve the quality of education. Her particular focus has been on technology in the classroom and use of the computer as an effective medium for sharing knowledge.

Diana T. Slaughter-Defoe, PhD, has been on the faculty of the School of Education and Social Policy at Northwestern University since 1977. Her research career has been devoted to understanding what distinguishes children who succeed despite overwhelming odds from those who become victims of their circumstances. She has been especially interested in characteristics of home environments that help children respond positively to severe challenges. She has not, however, restricted her research to home environments. Seeking to understand the interplay of home, school, and community on a child's development, she has followed cohorts of children from their infancy into adulthood —a difficult, rewarding undertaking that produces a richness of information impossible to obtain any other way.

The history of African American scholarly elucidation of the African American experience is long, distinguished, and exceedingly important. Slaughter-Defoe is a product and a perpetuator of that legacy. At the University of Chicago, where she received her doctorate in developmental and clinical psychology in 1968, she studied under and worked with some of those great scholars of the first half of the 20th century. Her research builds on and responds to their work. To keep their wisdom alive for new generations, she has written about the knowledge they generated, and she has extended the legacy by passing on the essence of their research to her own graduate students. She supports the infrastructure of African American scholarship by publishing in Black scholarly journals as well as the journals of her discipline.